Strange Things Happened on My Way to the Zoo

Mike Thomas

First published in 2010 by
Alison Hodge, 2 Clarence Place, Penzance, Cornwall TR18 2QA, UK
www.alison-hodge.co.uk
info@alison-hodge.co.uk

ISBN-13 978-0906720-73-8

British Library Cataloguing-in-Publication Data
A catalogue record for this book is available from the British Library.

Cover design by Christopher Laughton, based on a photograph by Paul Yockney

Book design and origination by BDP –
Book Development and Production, Penzance, Cornwall

Printed in China on paper produced with elemental chlorine-free pulp, harvested from
managed sustainable forests.

Credits

Photographs are reproduced by kind permission of: Paul Armiger, pages 134,
136 (left), 137, 140; Paul Crowther, pages 74 (bottom left), 85 (left); Croyde
Imagery, page 131 (bottom); Jenny and Sandra, page 160; Mike Hollist, page
144; Packet Newspapers, page 14; Colin Polkinghorne, pages 76 (mid), 92,
94; Michelle Turton, pages 54 (bottom), 62, 64, 66, 67, 68, 74 (top, bottom
right), 75, 76 (top, bottom), 77, 79, 80, 82, 83, 84, 85 (right), 86, 87, 90, 91,
95, 98, 100, 102, 103, 104, 107 (left), 109, 110, 116, 121 (bottom), 124, 129,
131 (top), 136 (right), 145, 152, 154, 155, 158; Bernard White, pages 130, 134
(left), 153; Barry Williams, pages 27, 35, 40 (top), 48; Paul Yockney, cover,
pages 29, 31, 33, 41, 43, 44, 49.

Contents

Acknowledgements   5

Early Daze   6

Tone Deafness is in the Ear of the Beholder   6
Chalk on My Hands   9
We are Sailing   15
The Furries at the Bottom of the Garden   16
A Step in the Right Direction   20

Marine Daze   26

Fur Coats and Wetsuits   26
Waving Goodbye to Mermaids   32
I See No Pigs   34
A Royal Soaking   38
A Royal Birth   39
Liberal Views   43
Politics Pay Dividends   44
Not a Fish Out of Water   47
No Sale Ahead   51
War and Peace   51
Full Sale Ahead   53

Zoo Daze   56

Daybreak   56
Bad News   64
The Strong Wind of Change   69
A Very Tasty Rainforest   79

Home, Sweet Home 82
And Sheep May Safely Graze 84
P… P… P… Pick Up a Penguin 89
A Loose Kneecap 91
The Coronation of the New King 96
Birds in Paradise 100
Where the Grass Might be Greener 103
Who's a Pretty Boy, Then? 107
Lame Kangaroos Can't Jump 111
Dining Out with a Friend 112
Blockbuster 115
Kept in the Dark 117
Mrs Griffiths' Roast Potatoes 121
Grinners in the Mist 123
A Time of Convenience 125
Marc's Arc 126
HQ was all it was Cracked up to Be 128

Paw Prince **129**
Once Upon A Time Big Cats Were Kittens 129
Putting One's Foot in It 134
Sheepdog 139

The Rising Phoenix **144**
Nice to See You 144
Where Have all the Cows Gone? 146
A Lion's Tale 150
Visitors from the Sky 153
Bangers and Mash 156

Back to the Future **159**
Beginning at the End 159

Acknowledgements

When we sold Newquay Zoo, my wife, Jenny, suggested that I should write about my many adventures in life so far. Being only semi-computer literate and inept at typing I wrote it longhand. Many pen refills, pencils and writing pads later I have produced *Strange Things Happened on My Way to the Zoo*.

I have been fortunate to have had help in composing it. My brother Richard found the photograph of Siloam in the archives, and listened patiently to me recalling my childhood days, correcting me when I made mistakes. Sue Coombes, my van driver at the Zoo and a compulsive bookworm, did the typing, retyping, retyping again... and tolerated my attention to detail. How she managed to decipher my writing, crossings out and pasting and cutting I'll never know. Michelle Turton, Marketing Manager at the Zoo, assembled the photographs, many of which she had taken. Jenny supplied tea, coffee and patience as well as proof-reading. We are still on speaking terms.

For permission to reproduce photographs I am grateful to Paul Armiger; Paul Crowther; Croyde Imagery; The Falmouth Packet; Mike Hollist; Newquay Zoo; Colin Polkinghorne; Michelle Turton; Bernard White; Barry Williams; Jenny and Sandra at The Donkey Sanctuary, Sidmouth, and Paul Yockney.

Through The Arc Trust we have been able to donate a sum of money to The Precious Lives Appeal to help build a hospice in Cornwall to provide care and respite to families and their children who have life-limiting illnesses. Further donations will be made to The Precious Lives Appeal from the sale of my book.

Early Daze

Tone Deafness is in the Ear of the Beholder

At the age of seven it seemed to me that getting married was an expensive business. The children in our street used to stand at the side of the road waiting for the wedding car to drive past, and stretched a white ribbon across the road to halt it. As it did, they waved and the bride and groom threw pennies and halfpennies for them to scramble after. Then they let it drive on. I made a lot of money this way when I was young. On a Saturday, when there were two weddings, I could make as much as sixpence.

I'm not sure if it was a Welsh custom or something that only happened in our village, but it was supposed to bring good luck to the newlyweds. It brought us good luck, because afterwards, before Mrs Baier Lewis closed her shop, there'd be a queue of kids clutching pennies, halfpennies and ration coupons since it was just after the War, buying their week's supply of sweets. Even if it was closing time, Baier Lewis always stayed open when she heard the wedding cars go past.

She was a deacon at Siloam Baptist Chapel, along with William Pryce, and when she retired William had to give out the hymn books and take collection himself. We all sang during collections, and so did William as he went from pew to pew. He sat in the front pew, below the pulpit, and dressed the same as the vicar, in a black jacket with a white handkerchief in his top pocket, pinstripe trousers, wing collared white shirt, grey cravat, waistcoat, fob watch and immaculately polished black boots.

William was bald... and the only tone-deaf Welshman I'd ever met. He sang at my baptism service when I was eleven years old, which involved me dressed in a white gown (I think it was a white nightie belonging to my mother), being totally immersed in the pool near his pew. While the vicar prayed for my soul, the congregation sang hallelujahs, and so did William. Albert Coker, farmer and choir master, said he sounded more like a cow giving birth than someone singing hallelujahs to preserve my soul. I didn't hear much of it, being more worried about drowning as I was plunged in and out of the water at each hallelujah. After the baptism we went into the vestry, where everyone kissed each other. That was the first and last time I kissed Mrs Baier Lewis.

Siloam Baptist Chapel.

Siloam nestled at the bottom of the mountain where, as a child, I played, walked in the forest and fished in ice-cold streams. It was there I learned to tickle trout by lying on my front, one arm in the water, hand cupped under the bank of the stream feeling for the fish, tickling it to keep it happy, before grasping it and pulling it out. My brother and I caught many fish that way, and cooked on a campfire they tasted wonderful. The mountain was the place of my formative years.

My mother, along with many relatives, is buried in the cemetery at Siloam, which looks out on to fields where, in spring and summer, sheep and cows graze, before the autumn colours give way to the crisp, white snow that covers the mountain, often before Christmas. I hoped my mother enjoyed these views. The lane to the side of the cemetery led to the cottage where she was born. She was home again.

The mountain stayed white with snow, untarnished by factories billowing out black smoke from chimneys, or cars turning it into muddy brown slush. It became scarred only by the footprints of foraging animals, people out on winter walks, and the tracks of our sleighs where we careered down steep and slippery hills, totally out of control.

It was my Siloam, my mountain, my Wales.

The chapel elders always sat downstairs, while 'our young people', as we were called, sat upstairs. My gran and Mrs Baier Lewis, who was now well retired from the deaconry, sat in the back row, where their pew was reserved for them. No one else dared sit there. It was the Holy Grail of Siloam, the forbidden fruit on the tree.

On Sundays, from her pew, my gran waited for me, and thrust a couple of mint humbugs – the brown and white stripy ones wrapped in clear cellophane – into my hand. She bought the sweets from Mrs Baier Lewis who only opened for an hour on Sunday mornings. Baier, a woman of the church with God-fearing ways, didn't really believe in being open at all on the Sabbath, but the money she took from those less God-fearing was too much of a temptation to resist. My gran obviously wasn't very God-fearing when it came to mint humbugs.

We waited, settled on those hard wooden pews where you were never meant to be comfortable, for the service to begin. William Pryce sacrificed all hymns in the name of religion, but 'Guide me O'er' was his greatest sacrifice. The organist played one tune, which was the one we all knew, while William went off in another direction, growling his way through five verses. The congregation got confused, and didn't know who to follow. Some went with the organist, and some with William. When the organist and her supporters finished, William and his lot were still going strong. Some of the congregation sat down, some didn't, and the vicar didn't know whether he should start his sermon or wait for the standing group to finish. I wouldn't have missed Sundays at Siloam for all the world.

Brychan Lewis, no relation to ex-deacon Baier, was the vicar. He was an erudite, intellectual man, whose command of the English language was impeccably delivered in a strong Welsh accent. No one slept while he spoke; at the faintest snore from someone in the hallowed hall, he'd shout his message and bang his fist on the lectern, spilling his glass of water, splashing and frightening all those in the front pews.

William Pryce often interrupted the sermon with loud 'Amens'. No one knew why, but it used to put Brychan off. You could tell, because he glowered down at William, who was quite oblivious to it, and pressed on regardless. 'Amen,' he'd say.

When Brychan finished, he came down from the pulpit, wiping his brow with the handkerchief from his top pocket, sitting as far away from William as possible. Apart from the removed brow-wet handkerchief, he was dressed identically to William. But he was not completely bald. He was on the top of his head, but there was hair around the sides, and long hairs stuck out of his ears which moved when he spoke.

When he died he left me his collection of poetry books.

After Sunday service, the elders had tea and cakes in the vestry, not being supporters of alcohol, believing it led down the road to hell and damnation. Brychan didn't go along with this line of thought, and enjoyed 'a heart warmer or two' when he came to our house for supper on Wednesdays before hymn practice at chapel.

One of his favourite hymns was 'We Will Gather at the River', and we generally gathered fairly close to it every Wednesday to practise. Only ours was more of a stream than a river. 'The beautiful, the beautiful river…'. No one can pronounce and resonate the word 'beautiful' quite like a Welshman. I love it, and even William Pryce was in awe of it.

'Love Divine' was another of Brychan's favourites, which was what I felt for Pat Roberts when she started coming to chapel. She was fourteen and beautiful.

We used to go for walks, hold hands and kiss in the peace and quiet of the country lanes. My 'Love Divine' shattered into tiny pieces when Pat and her parents moved to Birmingham. For a while I lost interest in going to chapel... that was until I fell in love with Stella Nott who was fifteen. Marriage was a distinct possibility. But my passion for poetry, later to be aided and abetted by the books Brychan left to me, overcame my desire for her.

I wanted to be a teacher, and that meant going to college, leaving Stella behind. My mother wanted me to be a vicar, but my father didn't mind what I did as long as it wasn't an overhead crane driver in a factory like he was.

Chalk on My Hands

So I went to college. In fact, I went twice. First to Goldsmiths in London to qualify as a teacher, then some years later I gained an Art Education Diploma at Cardiff College of Art and Design. It was there that I was intro-duced to the real world, and it was there that Ted Jenkins knocked the stuffing out of me.

I'd spent a whole term studying the impact of boutiques as creative art forms and, despite doubting its relevance to teaching, made the most wonderful model of a boutique, with moveable floors and walls, dim-mable lighting and sound effects. I was convinced it was worthy of a distinction at least.

Ted wasn't. He said it would make a lovely hutch for his rabbit. 'If you want to get your diploma, get real... a model is not a boutique.' 'Get real, man.'

But before Ted had a chance to get me real, my teaching career got off to a start in London. Kender Street was just off the Old Kent Road, within the sound of the Bow Bells, the heart of Cockney land.

The Big City was an exciting place to be in the sixties. It was the age of Flower Power, Mods and Rockers. I was a Mod. Musically, we were entertained by The Rolling Stones, The Animals and The Monkees, while The Beatles, who hailed from Liverpool, sent us all into frenzied delin-quency. Being on the short side, in order to look taller I wore boots with high heels and trousers that flared from the knees down. The Marquee in Soho and Raymond's Revue Bar in Piccadilly were favourite party places, while Lyons Corner House in Charing Cross Road was our favourite meet-ing place.

The Kray Twins were London's favourite underworld gangsters – real Cockneys, East Enders who, it was said, came from the Old Kent Road area. Since it was no distance from my school, I wondered if they had gone to Kender Street Primary School, which I called Gangster Kendergarten. There was a good reason for this. Late one afternoon, school had finished for the day, when the father of one of my pupils came to see me and asked me if I could do him a favour and store some boxes in my flat for him, 'Just for a couple of weeks mate, till I move 'em on, know what I mean.'

Sounded reasonable, after all he was one of my pupil's parents. But before he delivered the boxes, I heard on the local radio that a lorry had been hijacked in the Blackwall tunnel and its load of radios had been stolen. I wondered what was in those boxes. The hijackers were caught, the goods were recovered, and dad never came round with the boxes. For the sake of my preservation, and the fact that I am a coward, I left Kender Street after only one year.

I then spent three peaceful years teaching in leafy suburbia at Middle Park Primary School in Eltham, south-east London. Teaching wasn't very well paid at that time, so I used to deputize for Mr Beard, the school caretaker, when he went on holiday during the summer recess. It was a much better paid job.

*

I probably would have stayed another year at Middle Park, preferably as the caretaker, but returning home on my Vespa motor scooter after playing rugby one wet Saturday evening, I skidded and hit the traffic lights outside Blackheath station. A spell in hospital and a further period of recuperation gave me time to ponder upon the direction in which life's pathway was leading me. From my sickbed it didn't look too rosy.

London lacked forests, fields and streams to tickle trout in, and I desperately needed a mountain. I needed to smell the countryside, to lie in the grass and look up at the sky. To listen to the bleating of the mountain sheep, and see the skylarks swoop from the air. I wanted to catch the wind. I was homesick. So I resigned from the noble profession and went home to Wales.

'What on earth have you done to your face?' my mother asked me, which was when I realized the extent of the damage the accident had caused. It was further confirmed by an invoice I received a few days later from the council at Blackheath, requesting payment for new traffic lights.

'Don't tell me you're going to lie around all day doing nothing?' my mother said, as she watched me make myself comfortable on the sofa. It was less of a question, more of a command.

So I didn't tell her, but I did spend the next four months writing... two short stories and a play, which I submitted to fourteen publishers. The thought of being a writer was very appealing. 'Who knows, they might even make a film of my play,' I thought, in an idle moment of daydreaming. My mother wasn't convinced.

'First you wanted to be a teacher, now look at you, dreaming of being a writer. Just look what happened to Dylan Thomas, why can't you do something useful?'

'Dylan did, didn't he, he wrote *Under Milk Wood*?' But she was right.

I received fourteen letters from publishers thanking me for giving them the opportunity to read my scripts, but no thanks. Fourteen rejections. There was no future in writing, I decided.

I hadn't told my mother that I had applied to Cardiff College of Art and Design to do a diploma... something useful at last. I was accepted on the course since I was already a qualified teacher. We need teachers, Ted Jenkins said at the interview. Ted had a wicked sense of humour, and a gap between his two front teeth wide enough to accommodate another tooth. So I went to Cardiff each day and lived at home with my parents, and at the end of the year, despite the boutique setback, I got my diploma.

All too soon, it was a question of where to go next. Next happened to be my brother Richard getting married... in Cornwall. It was just what I needed, a wedding in Cornwall, where people went for holidays.

*

I had been to Cornwall once before. Mike James – we called him Sid – was at West Mon School with me. He was the only boy in Upper Six who had a car. An old Austin Ruby that had seen better days, but it was a car, an object to be revered by schoolboys. It hadn't been very powerful when it was new, and years of good and faithful service had taken their toll.

'I'm going to Cornwall, St Ives. Do you want to come?' Did I ever. It was school holidays, and I'd heard about St Ives.

We loaded up Clarice – that's what he named her – with the tent, two sleeping bags, a primus stove, cups, plates, knives and forks, groceries, two cases full of our clothes, and we were off. It was before the Severn Bridge was built, so we took the Beachley ferry, and our journey through England started at Aust, north-west of Bristol. We could have driven up to Gloucester, then down to Bristol, but that would have added another hundred miles to the eighty-seven thousand already on Clarice's clock. We didn't want to push our luck.

Austin Rubies had four gears – three forward and one reverse. Clarice was best in reverse. I thought Cornwall was downhill all the way. It wasn't. The journey had more than its fair share of uphills. When we got to the steep uphills, I had to get out and carry our cases while Sid turned the car around and went up backwards. And it rained most of the way.

The indicators on Austin Rubies were little orange plastic arms on each side of the car that lit and flicked up when you moved a lever on the steering wheel. The one on Clarice's passenger side didn't work, so every time we turned left I had to wind down the window and stick my arm out. Sid had his fair share of arm sticking-outs, because when we slowed down, which was often, he had to wave his arm up and down. When he wanted cars behind him to overtake, which was most of the time, he had to wave his arm back and fore. The rain poured in through the open window.

We had almost reached Exeter by the time it got dark, so we pitched our tent in a field, lit the primus and had a meal, followed by a wet night's sleep. It was still raining when we set off early next morning, and the windscreen wipers packed up. But it was possible to turn a knob on the dashboard and work them by hand.

Sid was a good driver, and drove slowly. During our journey from Devon to Cornwall we were overtaken by cars, lorries, pushbikes and two tractors. We almost got overtaken by a horse and cart, but were saved by a sharp bend in the road.

We arrived in St Ives by opening time, and sat outside The Sloop Inn with a pint of best bitter watching the fishing boats in the harbour on a warm, sunny evening. It was a wonderful holiday. It's funny how you only remember the good times.

*

When commitment time came for Richard, I packed my wedding clothes and my swimming trunks, relishing the thought of the holiday. 'It's October, not the middle of summer,' my mother said, but it wasn't called the Cornish Riviera for nothing, so my trunks stayed packed.

It was only to be a weekend, but that weekend in October 1967 held the promise that it would be a wonderful one. I'd saved enough money while at home, because my parents hadn't charged me any rent. My mother said that was because they thought I was only staying for a week, not a year.

With the saved money I bought a second-hand turquoise Mini without a scratch on it, but on reversing out of the drive to begin my journey I hadn't noticed that the gates were shut, and I ended up with a turquoise Mini with scratches on it. I intended to get a new bumper and some paint in Cornwall, since it took my father an hour to unbuckle the metal gates to let me out and I was now running late.

Six hours later I arrived in wedding paradise, where Diane, the bride-to-be, had arranged for me to stay bed and breakfast on a farm in Constantine owned by friends of hers, Roger and Gwen Collins. Bed and breakfast? What about dinner? Being there for two nights, on Friday I bought fish and chips in the village, and Saturday was no problem. Suitably wed, the blissfully happy couple led the way to a hotel in Falmouth for the reception, where we laughed a lot, danced a lot, ate a lot, drank a lot, and said it was the best day and night of the year.

For Richard and Diane it probably was. As for me, I woke up next morning with the daddy of all hangovers. And that was the day I was supposed to drive home to my job as one of the unemployed. Furthermore, the car still needed a new bumper and some paint. 'A packet of paracetamol and a tin of turquoise paint, please.' That should do it.

The bride and groom had gone on honeymoon to Bournemouth; I had a headache, a badly scratched car and no job. What was to become of a twenty-seven-year-old qualified, unmarried schoolteacher who didn't even have a girlfriend? I wondered where Stella was.

If I went back to Wales I'd have to pay rent. So I decided to stay on the Cornish Riviera. It was thanks to the bride and groom for getting married in Cornwall (which, as it happens, was where Diane was born), that I had a lucky break. A temporary teaching post at Wellington Terrace Junior Boys School in Falmouth came my way – a chance to get real. So much for Ted's rabbit.

*

All those years ago, when I went to Goldsmiths and had to find digs along with a hundred other students, reading the accommodation section of a local paper, I was amazed to find several adverts that had accommodation available but ended with... 'No coloureds or Welsh'. Until then I had been proud to be Welsh. Thank God I'm not coloured and Welsh. Shirley Bassey is. At the interview, just to be safe, I didn't say anything about being Welsh. I needn't have worried though, four of the eight staff were from Wales. Brychan Lewis said Welsh people are renowned for being the best miners, vicars, singers and teachers in all the world.

When the temporary job became permanent, I thought I'd made it! I dreamed of becoming a headmaster, eventually retiring to a cottage by the sea, preferably one with only a small garden for the wife to tend. The children would have been long gone and married, so there would be just the two of us to live comfortably off my superannuation. We could even go on a world cruise. I knew a headmaster who'd retired, and he and his wife did just that. They might still be on it, for all I know.

But first, I had to get through the next thirty-eight years. My classroom was in an annex building near the main school that a few years previously had been closed because it was substandard. The baby boom changed all that, and the annex came into its own again.

The toilets were in a stone-built, roofless building at the far end of the playground. Why did they build urinals without roofs, and why was this one at the far end of the playground? To go for a 'pee' in the depths of a Cornish wet and windy winter was a journey not to be undertaken lightly. On the plus side, it was a deterrent during lesson times, but playtimes saw queues of fidgeting boys, and some of them never quite made it.

There were wonderful views of Falmouth harbour, the docks, Pendennis Castle and, in the distance, St Mawes, visible from the very high windows. I was lucky to be tall enough to see out of them. The annex has long gone now, and in its place is an expensive block of apartments with amazing views.

At college I had been indoctrinated with radical views on teaching by radical, idealistic ex-teachers, who so impressed me that I wanted to be radical and idealistic too. I'd show Cornwall what good teachers are capable of. Chalky White, the headmaster, was at the retiring end of his profession, and radical idealism was not a view that he shared with anyone

The new classroom at Wellington Terrace Junior Boys School, Falmouth.

any more. He'd been at the school for thirty-two years, and generations of boys had passed through his doors without the need for all this 'new-fangled stuff'. 'You can do what you like when I've retired in two years time, Mister.'

But Mister was not prepared to wait two more years for his radical, ideological education to be put into practice. With the help of parents, local businesses and pupils, the classroom was transformed and the old desks were thrown out. The room was painted, partitions put in, new tables, chairs, cushions and shelves installed. A raised platform allowed the boys to see out of the high windows, and at last the harbour views came into the classroom to be enjoyed by all. 'We didn't know there were boats out there, Sir.'

It was a classroom of distinction – so distinct that the local paper took photographs and interviewed me. Chalky wasn't pleased about the discarded desks. 'Look at this… ,' he pointed to the initials 'B.C.' carved into the top of one. If this meant 'Before Christ' I was doomed. 'This is Brian Collins. Raymond Collins is in your class, and this is his grandfather. You are throwing away the school's history, Mister.'

A week later we threw the school's history into the rubbish skip, but not before Chalky had photographed it. There was a write-up in the local paper: several photographs; a bit about the parents and the boys helping; the support from local businesses, and praise for a forward-thinking headmaster. Chalky came down waving the paper. 'They think I'm forward-thinking.' He winked at me. Either that or he had developed an affliction.

The new classroom encouraged informal project work, and allowed for individual attention to the pupils. 'It's the way forward,' someone at County Hall said. We were going forward alright. It was not only the boys who benefited, but the parents became part of our community classroom, even joining in some of the lessons.

Many years later, after my 'bold experiment of informal teaching', as one local paper called it, I read that the government was calling for participatory, 'hands-on' teaching that promoted individual or group project work. I had been ahead of my time.

We are Sailing

One particular project, so much the way forward that it attracted the interest of the local community and the press, took place when Robin Knox-Johnston arrived in Falmouth to prepare for the first ever singlehanded, non-stop race around the world. *Suhaili* was the smallest boat taking part, and I took my class to see it in the harbour. We were going to enter the race, but not singlehanded. Seven groups, each containing five boys, prepared for the journey, which meant two boys were spare. 'Couldn't two of us have just a very small boat?' Raymond Collins asked. Reluctantly, they became coastguards, which, as I explained to them, was a very responsible job. Several yachtsmen, a yacht builder, a coastguard and a local lifeboat man came to talk to the class over the next four weeks. Real-life experiences were brought into the classroom.

Pupils learned to read maps and charts; take sextant readings from the sun, moon and stars; how to rig a boat; what weather and sea conditions might be encountered; what repairs could be done when necessary, and what supplies would be needed.

The race was 'imaginary reality' (virtual reality without computers) – a sailing experience in the classroom. Each group made a model boat, and each group made a smaller model of their model. Lists of supplies were drawn up, and items of clothing and weather gear were stowed in lockers. The day Knox-Johnston and other singlehanded sailors set sail, we pushed our boats out from Custom House Quay to cheers from some parents... four turned up. I wanted a cannon fired to start the race, but Chalky said we'd have to make do with a whistle. He blew it, and we were off.

Back in the classroom each group wrote a daily log of Robin's progress, and we used each group's model to indicate his position on large-scale maps. Whenever possible, and before his radio packed up, he kept us informed of his progress via the local coastguards. The Royal Naval Air Station at Culdrose sent us details of weather conditions to be expected, so that we would be prepared. More visits from yachting experts advised, among other vital details, what sails should be used to meet the conditions on each leg of the journey.

To Wellington School
with best wishes
Robin Knox-Johnston

Robin Knox-Johnston and Suhaili.

When Robin Knox-Johnston became the first person to sail single-handed, non-stop around the world in 1969, he sent my class of intrepid sailors his sleeping bag and a signed photograph of himself and *Suhaili*.

The class had learned not only about sailing, but about the world, the weather, survival, competition and, most importantly, how to work together to achieve success.

'This is better than school, Sir,' said Trevor Lawrence.

The Furries at the Bottom of the Garden

Chalky was becoming receptive to the 'new-fangled stuff', and basked in the praise from parents, governors and, occasionally, County Hall, the nerve centre of our county's education system. Yes, even they sometimes poked their heads above the parapet. Now that I was a successful teacher I was making friends in the trade.

Roger Butts, a teaching colleague, was about to marry Jenny, who taught at a nearby secondary school. The three of us often met for coffee after school, although I'd always been of the opinion that teachers *en masse* are pretty formidable. But when I was invited to be a guest at their wedding I was glad to be joining the formidable masse, and even volunteered to be a bell-ringer announcing the joyous occasion.

After the joyous occasion, we repaired to The Crag Hotel for the reception. Wedding receptions gave me a hangover, and although I was not one who enjoyed pain, when the now-betrothed were waved off on their honeymoon, we carried on celebrating for the rest of the weekend.

Soon after Roger and Jenny returned from honeymoon, my tenancy of the holiday flat in which I had been living was about to end, and I was to become homeless. However, the newly-weds, who had rented a cottage in Mawnan Smith, took pity on me, and invited me to be their lodger.

'Isn't it time you found a home of your own, like Richard and Diane?' my mother said, when I broke the good news to her on the phone. Despite this telephonic setback I took up lodging residence at Treave Cottage.

Roger's class at Wellington Terrace had guinea pigs, gerbils, spiny mice and deer mice, which in the term time were looked after by the children. During the school holiday, Roger took them home to Treave Cottage, where yet more homeless became lodgers.

'How do you manage when you go on holiday?' I asked him. This was not a good move, and was how I came to be in charge of a house, a garden, four male guinea pigs, two gerbils, four spiny mice and two deer mice.

They'd only been gone four days when things took a turn for the worse. Cleaning out the guinea pigs, I noticed that one of them had a wet nose and ran around in circles, which seemed an unusual thing for a guinea pig to do. When I checked their cage that evening, he was dead. Unfortunate, but these things happen. I buried him in the garden, then rang the vet, who came and injected the other three, 'just as a precaution,' he said.

The next morning, all three of them were dead. Precaution hadn't worked. I buried them and, near the four little graves, dug in four plants so that Roger and Jenny would know where they were buried. I was tempted to get four more guinea pigs, in the hope that they wouldn't notice the difference when they came home. Panic took many devious routes, but the four plants looked so good in the garden that I resisted the temptation.

I told the vet about the ineffective injections. But regardless of my comment, he went on to inject two gerbils, four spiny mice and two deer mice. 'It's a broad-spectrum antibiotic,' he said, which I took to mean that all would now be well. Perhaps it was a disease that only guinea pigs caught, and I was beginning to think this was so, because for the next few days nothing went wrong... no more deaths.

The spiny mice loved running around in a plastic wheel; it made me giddy watching them, but they were happy. Happiness comes in many forms.

The guinea-pig disaster reminded me of a story my brother told me. He had been cleaning his bike with a small bowl of petrol which he left on the floor beside him. His dog, Dinky, drank the petrol and ran around and around in circles, just like the guinea pig, but then suddenly he dropped on to the floor. I asked him if Dinky was dead. 'No, he'd run out of petrol,' he said.

When the two gerbils died the next day, I had a good sniff, just to be sure, before shaking them in case they were not dead. I buried them next to two plants I'd bought from the nursery down the road.

The following morning, the four spiny mice were dead. 'Perhaps they were missing their landlords,' was a thought that came to mind. Missing loved ones can be distressing. The vet was busy and couldn't come right then, but he advised me to bury them, which I did, next to four more plants.

Over the next couple of days, the two deer mice worried me, but they seemed to be alright. The vet thought that if they were going to catch it, whatever 'it' was, they would have caught it by now. How wrong he was.

That same day, one of the deer mice died. Taking no more chances, I took it into the vet to get it post-mortemed. After all, there was only one more chance to take. On the way home, I bought two plants – one for the mouse which was being post-mortemed, and one for the other one when it died. I put both plants on the window sill in the sitting room until they were needed. I've always liked plants in a house.

Outside, in the garden, were ten little bodies and ten colourful plants, such a pretty sight. Roger and Jenny were due home that evening, so I went to the pub, sat on the wall, looked out to sea and worried. By the time I got home they were there, having arrived early and, would you believe it, Roger was in the room where the animals had been. 'Where are they?' I pointed to the little deer mouse, running up and down the ladder in his cage, which seemed excited to see him. 'Where are the others?'

I waved towards the window, the power of speech having deserted me for the moment. 'So you've worked on the garden?' He followed me outside. I couldn't talk, but walking seemed alright. He looked at the ten mounds and ten flowering plants and, as speech returned, albeit hoarsely, I said, 'The vet injected them, but they all caught it.' He wanted to know what 'it' was, and why there were only ten graves. I said the vet was doing a post-mortem on one to find out what 'it' was.

Jenny brought us some coffee, admired the garden, and thanked me for the two lovely plants on the window sill.

A week later, a letter came from the vet saying that the deer mouse died of an infection, and it was therefore reasonable to believe the other animals caught 'it' and died of the same thing. He sent me his bill with the report… £360.00. I sent him a cheque by return. Holidays don't come cheap.

*

It was time for me to move on. My mother's words about getting my own house and settling down like my brother made me feel that that which was lacking in my life should be rectified… 'and the sooner the better,' she'd said.

So, with the help of a bank manager and a building society, I bought a fully furnished (except for a bed) terraced house, 25 Fore Street, Constantine, for £5,000.00. It was opposite the off-licence.

Someone suggested I should buy a waterbed, because they were all the rage for upwardly mobile people. Wanting to be upwardly mobile, I did. A waterbed is similar to a lilo, but bigger, and filled with water instead of air. It took a great amount to fill it, but at last it was ready to be slept upon.

The leaflet that came with it said the gentle rocking motion induced a soporific feeling, which was a prelude to a good night's sleep. But when I had a nasty bout of coughing, the gentle rocking motion was more like a buffeting by mighty waves in a force nine gale. I hadn't had it long, but one of us had to go. There was also concern that the weight of the water 'swooshing' about during any violent motion would cause a weakness to the now creaking bedroom floor. Violent motion had been experienced many times, and during such times the bed had been much admired.

Emptying it was a mammoth job, involving siphoning the water into the bath, which took a couple of hours to complete. When it was done, I put the empty mattress into the bin. Have you noticed, there's not much call for waterbeds these days? Conventionality led me to buy a brass bedstead and mattress, and I never looked back. Sleeping became a luxury again.

Furthermore, my teaching career was heading on a satisfactory course towards headship, until Chalky's retirement party. After his final farewell speech, which happened to be the third one (there'd been the school governors' private do, the staff party, and the big one with staff, parents and pupils), he said to me during the break for tea and cakes, 'I've been a teacher for forty-three years, Mister, and now my wife and I are retiring to a cottage by the sea.'

He'd been at Wellington Terrace Junior Boys School for thirty-four of those years. 'I taught their fathers and their grandfathers.' How exciting was that?

A war, different political parties in charge of the country during his time as head, and three recessions, had left him unscathed. It had had no lasting, damaging effect, and now here he was retiring on his pension to a cottage by the sea. In thirty-five years' time I could be his neighbour. Did all old headmasters and their wives live by the sea?

Soon after arriving home that day, I wrote my second letter of resignation from the noble profession. Although my school-teaching career was drawing to a close, education would remain a very important part of the rest of my working life.

*

But right now, another hangover was becoming necessary. The journey to Wales for my sister Sue's wedding was uneventful, which was more than I could say for the joyous homecoming. 'I never thought I'd see the day,

Michael, when your sister got married before you did. You were twelve years old when Suzanne was born, and you're still single. You're a good-looking boy, what's wrong with you?'

Hangovers are very unpleasant. Being married was a Welsh obsession, or at the very least a Thomas obsession. Don't get me wrong, I do enjoy weddings, especially when they are other peoples'.

So after the wedding, on my return to Cornwall, with mother's words ringing in my ears, I was ready to face my future, having convinced her that her boy was alright and would soon be looking for a wife.

A Step in the Right Direction

Having been in a position of unemployment once before, the prospect of this new, albeit temporary, self-inflicted setback to my career was not too distressing. I had no intention of going to the Job Centre. The people there didn't have my sort of job vacancies. Something would come up.

And it did one evening in the pub. A local farmer told me that soon milk churns would be a thing of the past, now that the Milk Marketing Board was turning to bulk tanks… modern and more efficient. 'That'll be the end of our bloody heritage,' he said, 'we will no longer see milk churns on stands outside farms waiting for the milk lorries to collect them.'

Having worked part-time on a farm and had experience of carrying full milk churns, especially the old steel ones, I had sympathy for the change… something a little lighter would be good. What bothered me though, was that milk churns, symbols of rural life, might never be seen by new generations. This would be like tearing the pages out of history books.

A week later I signed a contract with the Milk Marketing Board, and bought five hundred redundant churns. Lateral thinking, a few pints, and a chat to the landlord of the Bull Inn at Sonning, where I stayed while visiting friends in Reading, solved the problem of the vanishing churns and what to do with the five hundred.

'What about bar stools?' he said.

What about bar stools? Although rural symbols, in order to have the 'wow factor', the churns needed something a little more appealing to the masses. Milk churns are old, and 'oldness' is part of one's charm. Enhance their charm, accentuate their age, because old age can sometimes be attractive… I hope!

'Why not paint them?'

'No!'

'What about brass or copper… brass and copper are old, and I like brass and copper,' Dennis said. After a quick thirst-quencher or two, I knew a man who could do it, and promised to contact him.

Milk churns of all sizes got brassed and coppered.

Milk churns of all sizes from all over Britain got brassed and coppered, and then symbols of our precious heritage were sold world-wide as stools, sculptures and pieces of adornment. Although eventually I ran out of churns and so did the Milk Marketing Board, they will never now be pages torn out of a history book. The milk-churn story would forever be remembered and immortalized. I have one to prove it.

Meanwhile, no more churns meant no more money.

*

'You ought to get married and get a proper job,' my mother had said. Ever one for taking her advice, I did. Some time previously I had met Jan, who had two children, Ben and Holly, from her first marriage. In just over a year we married.

'There you are Mam, an instant family!' I told her.

I sold my house, and with the change, after repaying the mortgage and with money Jan had, we renovated a derelict cottage bought at auction.

The renovation came to the attention of *Ideal Home* magazine, which made particular mention of the concrete spiral staircase I had designed with an architect friend. Ultimately, like the milk churns, they became popular world-wide. I rented a factory, employed six people, and ran a

The concrete spiral *staircase – in the cottage (top) – was popular world-wide.*

Being introduced to Prince Charles at The Thorburn Museum and Gallery.

successful business manufacturing and installing stairways in Britain, Europe and the Middle East. Michael Caine had one, so did Stirling Moss. My company, Consculpt Ltd, supplied and installed stairways in Dubai for the Sheik Rashid Hospital; the largest spiral stairway in the world at the Chicago Beach Hotel, and the tallest in a mosque in Dubai main town.

*

But I had been trained to be a teacher and a designer. Owning and managing a factory that made stairways was not my chosen path in life. My direction altered when John Southern, owner of Dobwalls Theme Park, Liskeard, asked me to design an art gallery based around his collection of paintings by the Scottish Wildlife artist Archibald Thorburn. With help from a colleague, John Blackbourne, The Thorburn Museum and Gallery, an innovative interactive exhibition, became a popular educational and entertaining visitor attraction. It was opened officially by Prince Charles, and as the designer, I was introduced to him. From that time on I received many commissions to design and interpret exhibitions in museums and visitor attractions.

Being married with a family, was icing on the cake. Now I had a wife and two children for whom I was responsible. Caring for the children, and being cared for by them was, and still is, a wonderful experience.

Ben and Holly.

One thing I missed out on by having an instant family was not changing nappies, but I was happy to forego this pleasure. I soon discovered the joys of persuading a four-year-old and a two-year-old that fruit juice at breakfast time is for drinking not splashing each other with, and boiled eggs are best eaten with toast cut into soldiers, rather than 'eggy fingers'. I rediscovered the fun of making sandcastles on the beach, telling stories at bedtime, and the pride of watching them at school sports days and Christmas plays. At last I understood how my parents had felt all those years ago when I was young. Family life was enjoyable.

How excited I was when Jan became pregnant and told me that I was going to be the father of a new addition to our family. Soon I would be dad to three. Little did I realize the unimaginable sadness that was to follow. I was with Jan at the hospital during the seven hours of labour, while Mrs Jago, our neighbour, looked after Ben and Holly. When the baby's head appeared, I was taking deep breaths and shouting, 'Push!' When the birth was complete, I was as exhausted as the lady in the bed who had just produced a daughter for us and a sister for Ben and Holly.

Due to the difficult birth the baby was put in an incubator in a high dependency ward; not, I was told, an unusual occurrence. While Jan slept I went home, only to be called back to the hospital five hours later. The baby was having difficulty breathing. When I arrived the vicar was already there, and he christened Ami in the presence of Jan, me and two nurses.

The following day I registered Ami's birth. Then, in another office along the corridor, her death. The church service in a little chapel at the crematorium celebrated a life that had barely begun. For us it was no celebration.

But now, later in life, it has created an awareness of how precious life is and, for some, how short it can be. Perhaps Ami's death had been for a reason, and was to be celebrated. A good friend described Ami as a spirit who had adopted material form on earth for a short time in order to help us better understand our lives. Now she was a spirit again, and we should draw strength from her brief time with us.

When Ben and Holly went to university I realized her visit had indeed provided us with the strength, fortitude and understanding to make our lives sincere, kind, valuable and good. We will never forget Ami Thomas.

*

Over the years we moved homes several times, always within a five-mile radius, and when we bought Cott Farm, near Gweek, for me this was it... Utopia. We converted the cottage to provide a desirable and comfortable home for a family of four. It had six acres; a stream at the bottom of the garden, and a two-year-old donkey whom we inherited with the property. We called him Cyril, after the previous owner, Cyril Preen.

Our nearest neighbours were farmers, almost a mile away. The picturesque village on the banks of the Helford River had a pub, a shop, a tea-room, a chapel, and a seal sanctuary. That was where Ken Jones, an ex-miner from Tonypandy in the Welsh valleys, and his wife Mary lived, having established a rescue centre for sick and injured seals. I had first met them when they ran a café on the North Cornwall coast.

Ken's interest in seals started when he was out early one morning walking along the beach in St Agnes. In front of him, some distance from the sea, he encountered what looked to be a live animal. It was covered in cream fur. It was moving, and judging from the blood on the sand, was injured. He was soon to find out that it was a newly born seal pup.

And I was soon to find out that my formative years had not been in vain.

Marine Daze

Fur Coats and Wetsuits

Never work with children and animals. I had heard this many times, but didn't believe it, and when Ken Jones offered me a consultancy at The Seal Sanctuary, I was soon to find out why. When he and Mary left St Agnes, and bought land in Gweek to continue the work to which they were dedicated – a sanctuary for seals and any other creatures in need of care – they badly needed income. The Sanctuary's rescue work was already well known, and the establishment had become a popular attraction for the many visitors to Cornwall. It was a wonderful education facility about marine conservation.

Ken commissioned me to design an exhibition about marine life, pollution, and care of wildlife. As a teacher at Wellington Terrace School, I had established a 'hands-on' participatory education system for my pupils; in East Cornwall I had completed an interactive art gallery at a visitor attraction, and now marine life was about to become my oyster. I was going to work with animals, children… and a Welshman.

Ken told me that his early-morning walk along the beach at St Agnes had changed life's direction for him, and it was about to do the same for me. What did an ex-miner from Tonypandy know about seals? Not much. In fact, nothing!

But one thing was certain. All those years ago, on a beach in St Agnes, he wasn't prepared to leave a little cream-coloured fur bundle, with the 'biggest black, soulful eyes I'd ever seen', lying cut and bleeding where it would die. So he did what most people would do. Thinking that seals lived in the sea, he chased it into the waves, where salt water would soon heal its wounds.

Each time he did this, the pup returned, and flapped its way back up the beach. Seals' grace and elegance in water is not evident on land. After several fruitless attempts, much snarling from the seal pup, and much grumbling from Ken, he decided that the best course of action was to take it to his café home, treat its injuries, and return it later.

This was easier said than done, since there was a lack of co-operation from the pup, which resisted all attempts to be rescued. Teeth marks from seals provide a lasting reminder that they are wild animals not pets, as I discovered myself many times.

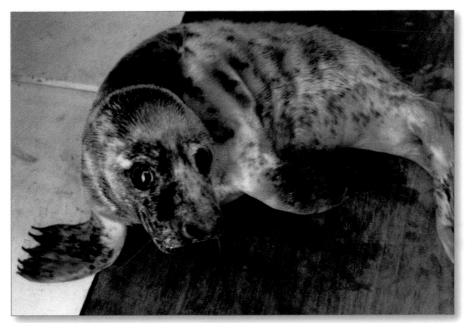

A rescued seal pup.

Ken's first encounter was such a reminder, but eventually he made it home with the reluctant patient wrapped in his now badly torn, probably beyond-repair, jacket.

This rescue was not successful. Cindy, as he named the little female, died. But it was to be the first of many rescues that happened at all times of day and night, mostly during winter, around the Cornish coast. The site at Gweek was ideally located for Ken's work.

*

Grey seals 'haul out' during the breeding season, on deserted beaches in fairly inaccessible rocky coves, and the rugged coast from Land's End to the Lizard in the south, and St Ives to Bude in the north, are favourite breeding grounds.

Pups are born mostly from October through till February, and for the first three weeks a new-born baby generally stays on dry land, covered in a creamy fur coat to keep it warm while its mother is at sea, feeding on enough fish for two, before returning to allow the pup to suckle the milky goodness on which it depends for survival.

After about three weeks, it begins to moult, and learns to catch fish for itself. It's a short weaning period that's fraught with danger. The early weeks are perilous for the defenceless pup, especially when storms generate monstrous waves that can wash it out to sea. Not having moulted, its fur coat would rapidly become waterlogged, and it would very likely drown, but if it managed to survive this ordeal it could be tossed around by the waves, before being thrown on to rocks or a beach far away from its mother. If this happened, cut by sharp rocks, exhausted, frightened and cold, it would face starvation.

*

Ken and his staff soon got to know the seals' favourite 'haul-out' coves, and kept regular watches during the breeding season. As news spread of the 'Seal Doctor's Sanctuary', so did calls about stranded seals, not just in Cornwall, but all over Britain.

And not only calls to seal pups in distress. Adult seals were sometimes cut by swimming close to ships' propellers; or they got caught up in fishermen's nets when they found what appeared to be an easy meal. Rescuing these adults was not only difficult, but extremely dangerous. However, all of them, of whatever age or size, had to be treated and given the chance to survive.

Obtaining supplies of the most ideal fish for food; treatment for illness and injuries, and replicating mother's milk for the young (then feeding them intravenously), were all part of the learning curve that Ken had gone through over many years, and imparted to his staff. I was eager to learn too.

Seals are susceptible to many diseases, especially if already weakened through malnourishment or injury. One particular disease, phocine distemper, almost wiped out the seal population around the coast of Britain.

It was during that difficult time, when the seal population was being devastated, that Ken was almost bankrupted because of the increasing expense of building more accommodation and treatment areas for these sick mammals. Thankfully, he survived, and the Sanctuary is testimony to his perseverance and dedication.

*

This was what I inherited when, along with other shareholders, I bought The Seal Sanctuary from him in 1988. He was a reluctant vendor; or, rather, he was a choosy vendor, and was determined to select carefully the prospective purchasers who would continue the work he started. We were the lucky ones.

A suitable deal was concluded, with me as Managing Director. My wife and I owned the largest share of the company. Other shareholders held smaller amounts, which ensured that Jan and I had a controlling interest in The Cornish Seal Sanctuary plc.

During my first winter in charge we rescued fifty grey seals. Many of them were newly born and orphaned, having been washed away during storms; some were young adults, which had suffered cuts and other injuries because they were not sufficiently experienced to be able to cope in bad conditions. Two we freed from being tangled in fishermen's nets, and

Amy: washed up and alone (left); safe at last (right).

several others had diseases, which proved to be curable. That year four died; nevertheless, this was considered a good success rate.

Seals have many sub-species relatives, and not all of them live in cold climates and seas. Sea lions, of similar shape, are darker in colour and, unlike seals, have external ears. They occupy warmer waters in America. Dugongs, which are much larger, are found in East Africa and Australia, while manatees – large and slow mammals – are found in freshwater rivers and lagoons in South America and the Caribbean. Then there are the tusked elephants of the seas... walruses, which inhabit Arctic waters around Baffin Island.

There were three sea lions at the Sanctuary. One of them, Rocky, blind from birth, came from a zoo where, being unable to entertain visitors, he had been 'surplus to requirements'. The sea lions became our permanent residents.

Rescued seals were first treated in the hospital. Here they remained for at least two weeks, depending on their problem, before being transferred to the weaning pools in preparation for a return to the wild in good health about six months later. Releases were always carried out on deserted beaches in calm weather. Those seals which, due to their injuries, would have been unable to survive in the wild became residents.

Visitors were allowed access to the hospital treatment rooms; talked to the staff about patients, and saw pups being fed, first with a milk sub-stitute, then with liquidized fish. In the lower pools, the seals were fed whole fish, generally sprats and mackerel. The feeding-time experience enthralled the visitors.

Ideally, prior to release, seals should be fed live fish, because in the sea that is what they eat. However, we don't live in an ideal world. I did it once, at evening time when the Sanctuary had closed to the public. Someone had been present who did not agree with feeding live fish, and that someone informed the local newspaper, whose maxim was that a story is never good enough until it is embellished and exaggerated. I read the article. Hanging was too good for me.

Shortly afterwards, I received a phone call accusing me of cruelty to fish. Despite countering the cruelty claim by saying that seals about to be put back to sea stood a better chance of survival by being retrained to do that which was natural to them, my accuser did not agree. A pity, because seals would 'turn up their noses' at deep-frozen dead fish in the wild.

To the majority of the British public the sight of seals chasing and catching live fish was not palatable. It was not a winnable argument. But my cruelty to fish did not lessen the Sanctuary's popularity, and the ensuing increase in the volume of traffic bringing visitors provided me with yet another problem which needed a speedy solution.

The Sanctuary was surrounded on three sides by an estate of bungalows, approached via four narrow roads. In busy times, traffic on all four roads was gridlocked, which was not an ideal situation for essential services such as fire engines, ambulances, police and doctors who needed immediate access.

Two unused fields provided an instant solution, and I organized diggers, lorry-loads of stone and gravel, and labour working under arc lights to create hard strips for car-parking. In my defence it provided a quick solution, but the prosecutors – the residents of Gweek – were horrified: (a) there was no planning permission for a car-park, and (b) they'd had a sleepless night during construction. I rectified (a) by making a retrospective application, but (b) took several months of humility and appeasement. In time I was forgiven, and the Sanctuary was adopted by the residents, who accepted it as an important facility, not just for seals, but for education and conservation.

*

But it took more than the residents' forgiveness for the Sanctuary's work to be appreciated and recognized as important by everyone.

A ship carrying oil had struck rocks off the Shetlands. Seals, fish and birds were among the casualties being washed ashore covered in oil. Such disasters were not unique. A similar problem had occurred when the *Torrey Canyon* foundered off the Cornish coast many years earlier, causing devastation to marine life and the environment.

Although our finances were limited, I sent a Land Rover and four staff to assist the rescue operation. My stepson, Ben, was one of the four staff, and he filmed, photographed and recorded the rescues of seals and oiled birds. This film became an important part of a conservation exhibition at the Sanctuary, and through our efforts and those of others, people are now much more aware of the dangers caused by oil pollution to sea creatures and the environment.

The foundation stone laid by Ken Jones, following that early morning walk in St Agnes, was being built upon by the Sanctuary establishing itself as a major conservation organization. For me, I was fulfilling a personal ambition.

*

Ken remained as a consultant for twelve months, then he decided to fully retire to his garden and ballroom dancing. I was left in control of The Cornish Seal Sanctuary plc. It also fell to me to undertake talks to the public at feeding times, a daunting task when upwards of three hundred people gathered around the pools waiting to hear about seals and the work of the Sanctuary. But apart from early 'stage nerves', this became an enjoyable part of my duties.

Courtney Eustice, an employee, was in charge of feeding the seals. He started as car-park attendant, but before working at the Sanctuary he had been a farmer. Although car-park duties had to be done, he was experienced at working with animals, as were many of the staff. He became a valuable multi-tasker. Courtney's work uniform consisted of a waterproof anorak, of which the right pocket was ripped; navy trousers tucked into black wellingtons, and a checked flat cap. (When I first saw him without his cap I was shocked to find that he was bald.) He fed the seals and I talked to the public about our work and the resident characters.

In Ken's time Courtney had developed a technique of skimming fish across the surface of the pool, splashing all within unsuspecting range. Most people enjoyed getting wet, and it was a technique he continued when I took control. These 'informal' feeding occasions often led to impromptu, unexpected events, and on one occasion I demonstrated how seals swallowed their fish whole, rather than chewing them, which would lose much of the nutritious value to the water.

Keeping a wary eye on Courtney I hadn't noticed that the seal which was about to take a fish was Dracula. He was blind, and had been a resident for several years. He could smell the fish in my hand although he couldn't see it. As I held the fish

Dracula waiting to bite the hand that fed him.

between my fingers, with my arm stretched over the pool, Dracula rose up from the water and took it whole, and with it most of my hand. Being blind he could not distinguish between fish and hand.

Withdrawing my hand from his mouth – it was now dripping blood and painful – I continued with the feed-time talk. Courtney fed the seals, splashing the audience, while Dracula banged his flipper against his chest to let us know that he wanted more. To the public it sounded as if he was applauding, and he was soon joined by the many visitors who appreciated such an entertaining demonstration.

While the visitors dispersed to the shop and café Courtney drove me to hospital for treatment to torn fingers. 'How did you do that?' a nurse wanted to know.

'A seal ate them.' Life was never without surprises, some good, some bad.

*

Leaning over Rocky's pool one morning, watching his ability to swim so unerringly when blind, I realized that people and animals cope with all sorts of problems. I discovered just how well when two visitors approached me wanting to adopt a seal for their daughter. They had been to the Sanctuary before, and their daughter had been a regular visitor. It was her favourite place and she spent much of her holiday, especially in winter, watching the seals at their 'haul outs' at Godrevy Head, Land's End and Lizard Point, before visiting the Sanctuary to enjoy their company.

They showed me a photograph of her. I was looking at an attractive woman in her early twenties who had short, fair hair, was wearing a pretty, floral-patterned dress, and sitting on a lawn near a bridge over a stream. I wondered where she was today.

She was dead. She had committed suicide. How well her parents were coping with such distress; but sometimes, something happens that is too much for one person to deal with. The adoption plaque at the weaning pool reminded us that she is still with her friends.

Waving Goodbye to Mermaids

Malcolm was in charge of the grounds, food preparation, seal rescues and releases... a sergeant major of our business. Rescues were happy times, but releases were better and had to be planned well in advance. They took place on deserted beaches, early in the morning, in calm weather. Previously, Malcolm and Ken had organized releases; now it was Malcolm and me.

The seals were rounded up from the weaning pool which had been drained, put into transportation cages, and taken to the chosen site by

Land Rovers pulling trailers of excited cargoes. It was a strange and wonderful sight for those up early and lucky enough to witness it. Releases were recorded on film and in photographs and diaries. Sometimes television camera crews came with us for news transmissions later that day.

The opened cages were lined up facing the sea while staff retreated up the beach. The seals, like all animals, were at first hesitant and reluctant to leave the security of their cages, but when they did, some flapped ungainly seawards, while others followed the retreating staff, wanting to go home to the safety of the Sanctuary.

A mass release required staff to remain at the site and observe for several hours, and the ultimate reward was the sight of the seals swimming to

Seals by the pool wait to be returned to sea.

where they belonged. Most of them 'belonged' not far away, and hauled out on rocky outcrops or in deserted coves. We followed their departure through binoculars, and one of the most exciting moments was to see seals join others in a cove some distance from the release site. Seals are social animals and live in large groups.

The coves were mostly ones that we had already logged as favourite haul-out areas where we would be keeping a watch nearer to breeding time. Who knows, some of their pups might one day need our help?

*

At the Sanctuary, I kept tape recordings of the sounds of the seals at their breeding grounds, and whenever these were played over the loudspeaker they elicited responses from our residents – mournful dialogues which at night were frightening experiences to the unwary. To the wary they were exciting, sounding as if the seals were singing.

Hearing these sounds one evening reminded me of the story of the young man in the congregation at Zennor Church, who heard what sounded like a young lady singing on a rock some distance out at sea. Her singing was so beautiful he swam out to find her and was never seen again.

It is said that sailors often saw mermaids sitting on rocks in the sea, singing and combing their hair. As the sailors' boats drew nearer for a closer look, the mermaids disappeared into the sea, and the boats foundered on the rocks.

At releases, looking through binoculars, I saw our newly released mermaids clambering on to rocks, stroking their heads with their flippers and, when the wind was in the direction towards the shore, you could hear them singing.

I See No Pigs

Seals are generally born in winter, which was always the busiest time in the hospital and for our rescue teams. December 1991 was busier than usual. Not all were new-born pups; many were young adults, weaned from their mothers and fending for themselves. They had long moulted their creamy fur coats in favour of grey wetsuits. It was unusual to find so many beached in such a distressed state, and most were ill, not injured.

Being older, they were also more difficult to handle, but when we did, examination revealed that many of them had poxvirus, known as 'seal pox'. The visible symptoms were swellings and ulcers on their flippers, faces and bellies.

Seal pox had been reported in populations in North America, but rarely in Britain. A grey seal was once reported sick with the disease in Cardigan Bay, Wales, in 1988, but the problem at the Sanctuary in 1991 was fast becoming an epidemic. Of the thirty young seals rescued in one month, twenty-one had seal pox in various stages of development. Despite the patients being kept in disinfected, individual pens, the pox spread quickly to the others. Seal pox was rarely fatal, and in time cured itself, but as a precaution we notified the County Veterinary Investigation Centre, since the Sanctuary's vet was concerned that the seals were not responding to any treatment we administered. The County Veterinary Officer, Vic Simpson, took biopsy samples under local anaesthetic from some of the seals, and sent them for examination to the headquarters of the Veterinary Centre in Tolworth.

Within days, seal pox was confirmed. So far none of the seals had died, although some now had suppurating blisters that were causing them considerable discomfort. By keeping them dry we hoped at least to be able to control the spread of these open sores, but a lack of written information on treatment of the disease meant we were sailing in uncharted waters.

However, seal pox was about to become the least of our troubles. Samples of ulcers removed from the lips of two of the seals revealed something more sinister: calicivirus. This had never before been discovered in animals this side of the Atlantic Ocean, and the available evidence of the damage of such a disease could have meant the end of The Seal Sanctuary.

*

Calicivirus was first discovered in sea lions in Southern California in 1932, then again in 1952 in the same area. The disease had also infected the pig population of some mainland states, particularly on the West Coast. While there was no substantiating evidence to indicate that the disease itself was fatal, the fact that pigs were part of the human food chain was sufficient to warrant wholesale slaughter of the pig population in affected states. This proved to be economically disastrous for the pig-farming industry.

On being alerted to the disease in our seals, and having only limited knowledge of the cause of the disease in pigs in America, the Ministry of Agriculture, Food and Fisheries (MAFF) took the easy route and panicked.

MAFF wanted to know the location of pig populations within a twenty-mile radius of The Seal Sanctuary and the Veterinary Centre in Truro, where possible contamination could have occurred. I was told that a veterinary officer from Tolworth Headquarters, during the course of his investigation, stood on the flat roof at the Veterinary Centre in Truro to see if he could see any pigs. Where were they hiding?

As far as MAFF was concerned it was a disaster of enormous proportions: one which, if not stopped immediately, could be as destructive as the Great Plague was to the people of London in 1665. Only this time it was pigs that were threatened.

Ulcers around lips on seal with calicivirus.

One Saturday evening a phone call from the Government Veterinary Centre informed our vet that all the seals in the hospital, whether or not they were infected with calicivirus, should be euthanased. Failure to comply with this request would mean that The Seal Sanctuary would be closed to the public.

Closure would mean no income at a time of high expenditure, and would have been more disastrous than the calicivirus itself. MAFF wanted to take the easy option, 'sweep the dust under the carpet', and pretend it never happened.

The initial reaction from the Sanctuary's board of management when I called an urgent meeting, was to comply with the request. However, as Managing Director, I was not prepared to accept this, since the job of the Sanctuary was to save seals, not destroy them. My response was just that. I was a lone, stubborn voice, unwilling to comply with the board's decision. There would have been a public outcry if the press had heard that we intended to euthanase healthy seals. Had push come to shove, I would have let it be known, but before I did the press picked up the story... from someone, somewhere.

My refusal to comply with the request, even when faced with closure and possible financial ruin, simply reinforced our commitment to the animals in our care, and gained us more public support. As the publicity for our determined commitment to saving the animals increased, the prospect of closure diminished, and we reached a compromise with MAFF.

The hospital became a 'no go area', and a barrier nursing system was adopted, which reduced the possibility of the disease spreading. Staff who came into contact with the hospital patients wore waterproof clothes and boots and disposable gloves and hats. The clothes were disinfected in the sluice room, and the staff had no contact with the public... or with pigs.

The patients were kept in dry pens, and staff had minimal animal contact except at cleaning and feeding times. These isolation conditions were in force for two months, although the animals' lesions healed naturally within a month and all but two seals recovered completely. Every precaution had been taken.

The two had to be euthanased due to secondary infections, which may well have been incidental and unrelated to the disease for which they had originally been confined. It became evident that neither seal pox nor calicivirus were life-threatening diseases, and were self-healing without the need for medical treatment. Although we had kept the seals in dry pens, it was likely that the healing power of salt water would have cured them in the wild. This was acceptable in large oceans, but not desirable in confined spaces such as hospitals, where contamination was more likely to occur.

*

Although the animals recovered totally, the source of the calicivirus in Britain was still a mystery. To find out more we investigated the outbreak in America, and made an interesting discovery. Following the disease on the West Coast in 1952, vigorous tests were carried out on many species of marine creatures, and calicivirus was isolated in an Opaleye perch – a Californian fish species.

Sea lions, which are partial to a fish diet and not too discriminating about what kind they eat, could have eaten them and spread the disease to others. But the link to pigs was tenuous, since pigs rarely came into contact with seawater, sea lions or Opaleye perch.

A breakthrough came when it was discovered that sea-lion carcasses had been used in animal foodstuff by a company on the West Coast which produced processed pig food. The food was distributed from their factory to depots along the West Coast by rail, for onward transportation to farms in the area. This went some way to proving the source of the disease. Sea lions had caught it from the Opaleye perch, become infected and their carcasses were used in the manufacture of processed foodstuffs for pigs. Deliveries were largely confined to the West Coast. If this was the case there would have been no danger to the British pig population from seals at the Sanctuary or, for that matter, from seals in our waters, since seal meat is not used in animal food products in Britain.

But we still had not been able to establish the source of the disease in British seals, since the Opaleye perch restricted its movements to Californian waters. However, it is possible that the disease is endemic in many fish and marine creatures, seals included, wherever they live. Since the seals that had calicivirus also had pox virus, the diseases may have been linked, because the symptoms were not dissimilar. It was possible that pox virus developed into calicivirus in extreme cases.

*

Had we complied with MAFF's request, it would have placed a heavy burden on the Sanctuary by making it responsible for the needless deaths of many seals. Although it had been a difficult time, Vic Simpson, County Veterinary Officer, together with a local vet, Noel Stewart, provided researched documentation about the evidence, symptoms, progression, treatment and cure of the calicivirus, which will be invaluable should there be another outbreak anywhere in the world.

Calicivirus had not disrupted the Sanctuary's daily routine, and visitor numbers continued to increase, which provided more income for our work in rescues, conservation and education. What was even more encouraging was that our income and visitor numbers were increasing at a time when Britain was in a period of recession and many companies were being liquidated or becoming bankrupt.

A Royal Soaking

An unofficial visit by royalty was on the cards when it was rumoured that the Duchess of York and her children, the Princesses Eugenie and Beatrice, were on holiday in Cornwall and might come to the Sanctuary. The Duke and the Duchess of York were in the process of divorcing, so an informal, unpublicized holiday was important for all concerned. A divorce on a royal scale was a very public affair and, should the visit occur, I was told that it was to be handled discreetly, with no prior publicity. I didn't even tell my staff. However, having already met Prince Charles, I was excited at the possibility of meeting more members of the Royal Family.

They say the best secrets are those that everyone knows about, and at the afternoon feeding time many of our visitors were newspaper photographers. By the time we reached the residents' pool, hoarse from talking and wet from Courtney's fish-throwing, I hadn't glimpsed any royal visitors. A photographer from a local paper was standing next to me. 'What a shame they didn't come, Paul.' He pointed over my head and, sure enough, in the direction of his finger, were the Duchess and the two Princesses. They were standing next to me.

And getting ready to throw fish, was Courtney. I saw the fish before the seals did; heard the splash, and felt the spray... but not before our distinguished visitors got very wet. Courtney, not knowing of the presence of royalty in our midst, looked over at me and shouted, 'Got you that time.' He smiled at his success. Our visitors not only smiled, they roared with delight.

Seals fed, all of us wet, the Duchess, two Princesses, a personal detective and I walked up to the donkey paddock. The 'girls', as mother called them, had brought Polo mints, donkeys' favourite sweets. For several hours the royal group mingled with the visitors. Before they left I presented the Princesses with a cream, furry toy seal each, as a reminder of their visit to The Seal Sanctuary.

The next day the royal party caught the train to London, and the photograph in the papers, taken at Truro station, showed the Princesses cuddling furry seals.

*

The Duchess and I had several things in common at this time. We were both at The Seal Sanctuary; we had both got wet at Courtney's hand, and we were both getting divorced. After seventeen years, Jan and I separated.

Although Ben and Holly are my stepchildren, they had been with me for seventeen years. I am very proud of them. I might not have a wife for much longer, but I still had two children, not blood-related, but in every other way I am their dad, and always will be.

Not everything that at first seems disastrous, turns out badly.

A Royal Birth

Any day now, two momentous events were about to happen. The first was the receipt of divorce papers from my solicitors; the second was the birth of a seal pup. One was a time of sadness at the end of a relationship; the other was the happy prospect of a birth – a new beginning. It was up to mum and the baby to do the necessary when required.

So we waited. Some doubters among the staff didn't believe it was going to happen, but, as a precaution I had transferred the seal, which looked very pregnant, to an isolation pool some days ago.

Looking pregnant was more than just being fat. She had a strange look about her (probably not the most scientific way of establishing imminent birth), and her rear end seemed to have dropped a little (not a means of establishing imminent birth in a human!). Teats were not evident; they only became so shortly before a birth. The vet couldn't perform a scan, since his machine would not give us a picture on account of the thick skin and depth of body fat. These were two of the disadvantages of being a seal when proof of pregnancy was required.

After a week of inactivity and lack of action from mother, the doubters on the staff wanted to transfer her back to the larger residents' pool. I wavered a little, but held firm.

A big seal in a small pool was not ideal, but if the birth happened she needed solitude and an empty pool. The pup, in order to avoid drowning, would have to be born on dry land. We drained the pool... and waited. When her waters broke it seemed the birth was about to happen and my motive justified.

We waited... and waited.

We'd played the waiting game so far, we wouldn't give up now. The labour period had begun; mum supplied all the action, but still no pup appeared. She was obviously in pain and distressed. Reluctantly, we decided she needed our help. Courtney, having been a farmer and having delivered calves and lambs on many occasions, was looking forward to delivering a seal. With his jacket off and sleeves rolled up, he said, 'This will be my first seal.'

The reason for the delayed birth soon became apparent. The umbilical cord had become tangled around the pup, preventing its entrance into our world and, because the female's waters had broken too early, the passage out, which should have been wet, was dry. But through patience, soothing words of comfort and careful manipulation, Courtney eventually completed a successful birth.

In the wild, such a problematic birth usually resulted in a stillborn baby and, very likely, a dead mother. We could not have let this happen. Courtney moved the pup close to mother to enable it to suckle from her teat, since the first milk, containing colostrum, was a vital first meal which would provide natural immunity from infant ailments.

Mother, however, did not co-operate. She turned and bit into the pup's head, trying to kill it, which was probably due to our intervention by

Duchess shortly after her birth with blood on her head (top), and her first day in the hospital (above).

transferring human scent on to the animal. While hand-rearing was not ideal because it could destroy the animal's natural wild instincts, there was no alternative. The pup had to be given a chance to live. I dragged it from the female and hurried out of the open gate with the precious bundle wrapped in towels. I heard the crack of the broom handle with which Courtney was defending himself and me against a ferocious female as her teeth broke it in two. A breathless, but safe, car-park attendant-cum-seal midwife followed me safely out, and slammed the gate shut as an

Duchess, having put on weight and soon to go to the weaning pool.

angry seal hurled herself against the bars. A timely reminder that seals are wild animals.

A long overdue seal pup was cleaned; rubbed with rough towels to accelerate circulation; fed goat's milk as a substitute for its mother's first and vital meal; injected with a broad-spectrum antibiotic (where had I heard that before?), and put into an incubator for warmth... a precaution rather than a necessity. In the wild, close proximity to mother would have been sufficient, since it had its own fur to withstand the cold of winter. This was spring.

We had a live seal pup and a live mother, which, having settled and become less aggressive, was transferred to the company of those in the residents' pool. There seemed to be no pining, no sadness and, fortunately, no ill effects.

Our pup was a baby girl, which, with due regal pomp and a lack of imagination, we named Duchess. Courtney wanted to know why we didn't name it after him. 'Girls are not called Courtney... are they?'

I became Duchess's surrogate mother, and she even followed me around the hospital at cleaning time, just like a child follows its mother. When she was six weeks old we transferred her to the weaning pool in the company of other seals which would be released to the wild early in the autumn. Having been closely exposed to human behaviour she needed to become a seal. She was a special case and had to be monitored, for unlike the others she had never been on a beach or seen the sea.

When autumn came, and with it release on a deserted beach, without so much as a backward glance in my direction Duchess swam through the waves. She was behaving as a normal seal, which was encouraging. Malcolm said I looked bloody silly waving as she swam away, especially since the release was being filmed by television cameras.

That evening, during the local news programme, I saw me waving goodbye to my mermaid.

*

Not all births at the Sanctuary had such a happy ending as Duchess's.

When a female sea lion, which we hadn't known was pregnant gave birth, we were totally unprepared for it. If we had known, we would not have interfered out of choice, but would have observed, with possibly a less damaging outcome. We found the dead baby and a grieving mother which, for several days, carried her pup around, not allowing any of us near.

It became necessary, both for her well-being and for the prevention of possible disease, to remove the body, which was easier said than done. An angry sea lion, like an angry seal, is a dangerous animal. We needed to find a way to remove the body without danger to staff. The viewing platform above the pool provided our hope for a safe retrieval.

To one end of a long pole we attached a wire that dangled down, ending in a loop, which, when we located the body, could be tightened around it and pulled up. When the female saw what was happening, she rushed towards it, pulling it back to her. She was quicker than we were. A variation and improvement to our 'fishing rod' was called for, which was how we came to modify the pole as a see-saw, balancing it on a central fulcrum. The line, dangling down, was manœuvred around the body and tightened, and several staff put their combined weight on the free end of the balanced see-saw.

The body swung out and up in a wide arc before the female was able to reach it to pull it back. The momentum carried it above our heads and behind the viewing deck, where it landed on the grass. Not the most delicate and dignified way of retrieving a body, but a successful one.

We had the pup, but the desperate cries of the female said that she didn't. A rubber toy sea lion from our shop provided a solution, and it was smeared with the scent of the dead pup and lowered down to her. She leapt for it, a suitable substitute having been found for the time being. But now the dead baby, several days old, decaying and smelling, had to be examined to find the cause of death. Our vet was more than a hundred miles away on other business when I told him what had happened. 'What could we do?'

As he explained, it was not what 'we' could do, so much as what 'I' could do. I had never performed a post-mortem, and was not keen to do so now.

'What's it like to be a managing director?' he asked.

Suitably attired in hospital hat, face-masked and with scalpel poised, I listened carefully to his phoned instructions. The first cut, to reveal the lungs, was excruciating. I felt every incision. I could never be a surgeon.

He told me what the lungs looked like and, with a few, hardly deft moves, they were sitting in my hand. He asked me to squeeze them

Our sea lion had her baby at last.

gently. Had the pup been alive when it was born, there would have been a residue of air in them which I would have felt... a bit like a balloon before it was totally deflated. No air meant the pup had not breathed.

There was no evidence of any other problems; no injury, no disease, no malformation, which showed that the pup died of natural causes, and meant that there was nothing to prevent a future successful birth.

Liberal Views

The Seal Sanctuary's fame had spread to the seat of government, the Houses of Parliament, no less. A 'hope-to-be' future Prime Minister, Paddy Ashdown, leader of the Liberal Democrats, was visiting Cornwall, campaigning on the run-up to the General Election. The

Paddy Ashdown (now Lord Ashdown) wooing the floating voters.

Showing Paddy how to do it.

Sanctuary was on his list to visit, and when he did he helped me feed the seals, accompanied by the flashes of the photographers' cameras, all hoping for the elusive scoop!

'Never a day goes by,' I said to my mother on the phone. She knew what I meant, being a past-master at finishing my unfinished sentences.

We hadn't been much help though, because the Lib. Dems only came third. But the photographs that appeared in the national newspapers showed how much the floating voters appreciated his visit.

Politics Pay Dividends

It wasn't only the Lib. Dems that knew where we were. Someone in Portugal did.

A fur seal, a native of the Antarctic, was found in the harbour of a fishing port, facing not only danger from other boats, but danger from the warmth of the Mediterranean water. One explanation for its presence in Portugal was that it had been found in nets by fishermen, kept on board, fed and treated as a pet. On reaching the harbour it had been dumped overboard, since bringing it in to port was illegal. This was just a theory. It may well have come from an aquarium, but no one was saying, and the true facts would never be known.

However, after an MOT by a Portuguese vet, we had it flown to Bristol and then, with the help of the RSPCA, driven to the Sanctuary. After a couple of weeks of quarantine and some tender loving care, the wanderer was taken to Scottish waters. From an identification tag we put on it we heard that it had been sighted several months later with other fur seals off the Shetland Isles. The Sanctuary had again provided a safe haven for a marine mammal that needed help.

*

Two other marine mammals needing help were in America. An aquarium in Cape Cod was closing due to lack of finance. Its two sea lions needed a home. I sent a fax offering them a home in Cornwall. There was no possibility that the two sea lions, which had been born in the aquarium and were used to doing 'tricks' at public displays, would survive in the wild, because they were used to people, relied on them to be fed, and probably enjoyed their company. To have put them to sea would have been irresponsible, cruel, and probably the cause of their deaths.

There were only two options. One was to euthanase them, which was not an easy decision for anyone to have to make. The second – the reasonable one – was to find a suitable home. But despite pleas from the aquarium, no one in America had come forward with a rescue offer. In Cornwall we did, but time was running out.

The best endeavours of the aquarium in Cape Cod and The Seal Sanctuary in Gweek had not reckoned with the lumbering, time-consuming machinations of government bureaucracy. The next couple of weeks turned into a race to save two healthy animals from death by lethal injections. While an airline offered to fly them to Britain free of charge, and the aquarium offered to send two staff to ensure their care during the journey, a Certificate of International Trade of Endangered Species (CITES), needed for importation, was becoming more difficult to obtain than a win on the football pools.

While the plight of two sea lions in America drew scant attention from the authorities, people who cared, on both sides of the Atlantic, waited anxiously. In Britain the Conservatives had won the election, and John Major was Prime Minister. Was the political tide about to turn for two sea lions from America? We'd arranged the transportation by a sponsoring airline; keepers would travel with the animals; forms had been filled in, but we still did not have the vital certification from the government department necessary for their importation.

Where were their passports? People from all walks of life and all parts of the country came to the Sanctuary. During a feeding-time talk to a large crowd of visitors, I spoke of the plight of the sea lions, and said that if Mr Major could help us now it would be the first useful thing he'd done since he became Prime Minister. Two weeks later a telex arrived saying the Prime Minister would do all he could to help speed up arrangements for the transportation of the sea lions from America... 'and he had done some

Courtney introducing himself to Ursa and Pepper.

other useful things'. Talking works wonders, and actions speak louder than words. Two sea lions will be forever grateful to the Tories.

We met Pepper, her daughter Ursa, and two keepers off a flight from America at Heathrow airport late one evening. We collected the CITES document from Customs Control, and the long journey to Cornwall began. The quarantine period was to be at the Sanctuary, and the sea lions, having suffered no ill effects from the flight, were settled for the final leg.

A convoy of four vehicles arrived in Cornwall in the early hours of a dark morning, where my staff had added a few final touches... a large rubber ring, a beach ball and a plastic snake, in a welcome-home swimming pool.

Rather than create a disturbance in the remaining hours of darkness the sea lions stayed in the travelling crates until daylight.

The story of Pepper, Ursa and the work done on both sides of the Atlantic to save them, was of national interest. By the time we opened the travelling crates, the Sanctuary was packed with the press and media wanting the best pictures and the best story. Pepper and Ursa did not disappoint. They swam eagerly in the pool and played with their new toys.

Barry Williams, a BBC cameraman friend of the Sanctuary and his wife Joyce, had met us at Heathrow airport and filmed the journey of the sea lions from the time they disembarked from the plane to their first swim in their new home, where they eventually provided entertainment for our visitors. Being used to 'doing tricks' at the aquarium, this became part of their daily routine. Animals, like humans, are creatures of habit, and performing 'tricks' was part of the sea lions' behaviour pattern.

A new country and a new beginning culminated in a sea lion pup's birth to Pepper some months later. She had been pregnant before leaving the States. Three for the price of two.

John Major will always have a place in our hearts. Had the pup been male we would have called him John.

Not a Fish Out of Water

It wasn't only sea lions and seals that occupied our time and delighted our visitors that summer. When staff on weekend duty received an early-evening call from surfers on a beach at Godrevy, near Hayle, a momentous animal rescue took place. A young dolphin had been washed up alive, cut and distressed.

Our emergency team reacted spontaneously, and our vet, with assistance from Matt, my secretary, drove in a rescue Land Rover with a trailer to the beach fifteen miles away. I followed in another vehicle, while staff made preparations at the hospital, moving two bewildered seals from one of the pools to prepare it for a dolphin.

The rescue of Spirit.

During the journey back to the Sanctuary the dolphin was continually hosed down, and the trailer was packed with ice from a freezer in the cold room. Although the dolphin was in a very weak state, it was still alive when we arrived at the Sanctuary. The next few hours were the most critical. Animals suffer from stress, and this young dolphin had been stressed enough through injuries and being manhandled on a fifteen-mile journey.

Our vet, James, treated the wounds, which luckily were superficial; he injected the dolphin with, by what I now knew was broad-spectrum stuff, and fed it intravenously with energy-giving electrolyte liquid. Stabilized, the dolphin was taken to the prepared pool; lowered into the water, and supported throughout the night by wetsuited staff and volunteers who held it to avoid water getting into its blowhole. We didn't want the dolphin to drown having survived this far.

There was much conversation that first night, and for many nights thereafter, since talking to the dolphin kept it calm and helped to reduce the level of stress. When the first light of morning appeared the dolphin was still with us. Its fighting spirit, and the dedication of our staff, had kept it alive through the night.

For the next week, night and day, staff and volunteers held 'Spirit' until he was strong enough to support himself. For the first few days he was fed liquidized fish supplemented with energizing fluid, through a tube passed down his throat, into his stomach. Great care was necessary to

Spirit – fit and well, and ready to go home.

ensure that the feeding tube was correctly placed into his stomach – a difficult process with an animal that didn't understand he was being helped. When he had regained sufficient strength, he was transferred to a larger pool and did what dolphins do naturally: he swam and caught fish.

The weather was predictably fine, and nights were warm, but it was still necessary to maintain nightly vigils. There was no shortage of volunteers. For Spirit's benefit and ours we played music, sang and had barbecues. My most enjoyable memory from that time is of swimming with him and holding fish high as he leapt out of the water to take it from my hand. Spirit was a fit dolphin again.

Although he had become the main attraction, with many visitors travelling hundreds of miles to see him, when he was ready to go home we enlisted the help of Royal Naval Air Station at Culdrose. Dolphins live in the sea, and that's where Spirit was bound. A naval helicopter had reported a sighting of dolphins just off Lizard Point. They live in social groups called pods, and that was his destiny. Had we not found the pod, his reintroduction would probably have been in vain. So no time was lost, in case the pod moved on.

Culdrose Naval Air Station lent us two large inflatable boats. Some of my staff, a dolphin and three air naval personnel motored out of the Helford River seawards, directed to the location of the other dolphins by a naval helicopter. Keeping our distance, so as not to frighten them away, Spirit was lowered from the boat. For a while he circled us, and gradually, when the helicopter moved away, the curiosity of the others drew them towards us. Spirit was back with his kind. When we saw that he had joined them we turned for home, leaving the helicopter to track the pod's movements and film the dolphins as they disappeared further out to sea. For us, it was a spectacular triumph which we would long remember.

A local resident penned this poem in appreciation of our effort.

Dolphin

When we hear of Sarajevo and the slaughter on its streets,
Where innocence is sacrificed to partisan conceits.
When we read of other conflicts spreading turmoil round the globe,
The world seems wreathed in sorrow and a blood-encrusted robe.

Against this torrid background, one could willingly concede
That the saving of a dolphin might seem trivial indeed,
But I clutched upon that story as a man would clutch a rope
Were he deep beneath the water, losing consciousness and hope.

For I needed that assurance, that elusive chink of light
Where the milk of human kindness thrust the shadows out of sight
It's a precious time for heroes, we should prize them where we can,
On their mercy-mission convoys or a strip of Cornish sand.

Two lifeguards with a body in a battered dolphin skin,
But neither saw him less than part of valued kith and kin,
No pair of guardian angels could have offered more than they
'Til Gweek provided comfort in its dedicated way.

And there began the vigil through the night's foreboding stare,
A struggle where compassion fought the efforts of despair;
I don't know how they did it but I know the reason why
With the stubbornness of humans, they refused to let it die.

We have these varied talents and we use them as we will,
For honour and for triumph or to brutalize and kill.
As a doctor wields a scalpel and a villain wields a knife
So a man can slay another or can save a dolphin's life.

From the sanctity of Cornwall, it's effrontery to preach
Or to liken Sarajevo to a sandy Cornish beach.
But somewhere in between us, such humanity has died
And compassion is a dolphin left to flounder on the tide.

No Sale Ahead

During my time at the Sanctuary we had done a great deal to increase the facilities for our visitors and the mammals in our care. So much so, that a leisure company, specializing in aquaria and marine-life attractions, expressed an interest in buying Cornwall Seal Sanctuary plc. Their examination of the company's accounts, readily available to be seen by the public at Companies House, together with their anonymous visit to the Sanctuary, prompted an offer to be made.

While one day the company would be sold in the interests of the shareholders, this was not that day. Much more conservation and education work needed to be done before that day dawned. The shareholders had so far kept their faith, and we were now in a sufficiently strong financial position to be able to pay dividends. Furthermore, Jan and I, although separated, not yet divorced, owned twenty per cent of the company – enough to stop a sale. We stood together in our desire to retain the Sanctuary, and at a board meeting on the matter I made my case for its retention.

Fortunately, at a shareholders' meeting, the offer was rejected. Our work would continue... and was I glad it did... especially when an international incident needed to be dealt with.

War and Peace

A message on the answerphone at the Sanctuary, timed at 7:30 am GMT, was from a British vet working in Amman, Jordan. He knew of our work with marine mammals and wanted advice.

It had been a popular year for sea lions so far, and this incident was no exception. A fisherman had brought an injured sea lion, caught in his nets, into the veterinary centre in Amman. It had a deep cut on its shoulder, possibly caused by a boat's propeller, and required urgent attention. The vet envisaged no problem with repairing the wound, but was hesitant about the type and dosage of anaesthetic to be given. The time difference was a critical factor if the animal was to be saved, and Amman was two hours ahead of British time. Already it was 10:30 am there. If the wound was bleeding, speed was essential, so a message was faxed to the veterinary centre with the required information.

Anaesthetizing any animal can be dangerous. Too much could kill it, but too little would mean that the animal was not fully sedated and dangerous. Marine mammals are particularly prone to stress from anaesthetic, so the type and dosage was vital. Several hours passed before a message was received saying that the operation had been successful.

One lucky young sea lion would once more go to sea. But the direction in which it should go was a bit of a dilemma and needed clarification. Sea lions are not indigenous to that part of the world, so it must have been an

Cott Farm (above), and my favourite garden seat (left).

sandwiches, drank wine, and congratulated me on my 'soon-to-be-made new appointment', wink, wink. The sale was finally concluded when I put my signature on a document in the purchasers' solicitors' offices in London a month later.

After signing, hands were shaken; the purchasers and board-member vendors ate sandwiches and drank champagne, while I took a taxi to Paddington station to catch a train home. This was not my celebration.

All shareholders had been given the option to take the share sale money in cash or in a combination of cash and preferential shares. Since I was to be Managing Director I decided to take a third in cash and two-thirds in preferential shares, which, when I told them of my intention, took the old board and the new board by surprise. 'Fancy him not taking the cash when he was not in favour of the sale.'

On the train home I read my new contract of employment. Then I made my way to the dining car, and had dinner and a half bottle of 'very expensive' wine. For me, little had changed, except I was now no longer an owner of the Sanctuary, but I was financially stable and still in charge.

The next day, as usual, I drove to the Sanctuary and walked into my office to find, sitting at my desk, the new company accountant. He shook my hand and gave me a letter. Probably a letter welcoming me to the company.

It wasn't. It was a letter telling me I was sacked. This had been the shortest job I'd ever had. He stood there while I cleared my desk, then drove me home in the company vehicle.

With my donkey, Cyril.

In the driveway he helped me unload; shook my hand again (was there no end to it?), turned around and drove away in the company vehicle.

*

I was carless, jobless and wifeless.

But I had Cott Farm, a donkey called Cyril, a retriever called Nick, and Gingerman the cat. In the safety of the kitchen, I made coffee; looked at the cheque that had arrived in the post that morning; examined the purchase-of-shares document, and pondered life's direction yet again.

Zoo Daze

Daybreak

Getting divorced and sacked in the space of a few months were not experiences I'd like to repeat. My confidence had received a few body blows lately. But from being a depressed optimist who felt that every silver lining had a cloud, I was beginning to feel a little more cheerful. My dusk was turning into dawn. The shares I'd taken instead of cash for the sale of the Seal Sanctuary had doubled in value; a new romance was a possibility, and my bid to buy the lease of Cornwall Animal World from Restormel Council was being considered.

Following the sale of The Seal Sanctuary, for the first time in my life I felt financially secure. I no longer received weekly letters from my bank manager begging funds to prop up my leaning account. I wouldn't say I was rich – divorces don't come cheap – but I had a bob or two, and there's no doubt that the money in the bank boosted my confidence. Being a depressed optimist who dared not look up, when I did I saw a cloudless strip of silver at last.

I was not lonely at Cott Farm. During college holidays Ben and Holly came to visit, and friends often came to dinner. Cyril, Nick and I became best friends, and were good company for each other, while Gingerman did what all cats do best: he slept.

Before we bought Cott Cyril had lived with cows. He thought he was a cow. The only difference was, he didn't moo or give milk. However, in the fields, just like them, his head was down and, like a well-honed lawnmower, he devoured the grass at a fair rate. Cows have two stomachs, and are able to cope with rich grass. Cyril had only one, and, especially as he got older, found it all too much for him. Thinking he might like company, the neighbouring farmer suggested that I could let Cyril run with his cows. However, after a couple of days I went to see how he was getting on with his new friends. He wasn't. The rich pasture – cows' manna from heaven, a donkey gourmet's delight – had taken its toll. He was bloated and could barely walk.

A staggering donkey that I had to lead home across two fields, supporting his head on my shoulder, was not, at the time, my idea of an ideal pet. We made it though, and I shut him in his stable on a diet of complete starvation. 'No more friendly cows for you my lad, a visit from the vet is what you need.'

He didn't like John Head, the local vet. Whenever I called John out he had to arrive disguised in a hat, wearing an overcoat. Anyone approaching Cyril's stable resembling John, and Cyril was nowhere to be found. A couple of years earlier John had been the vet who castrated him, and he never forgot or forgave. Who would?

But he liked me. Whenever I was out in my new second-hand Daihatsu four track Cyril recognized the sound, and on my return would be waiting in the corner of the paddock for me to arrive. There would be no peace until I went to see him to say hello or goodnight. That's what friends are for.

*

And talking about friends, I met Jenny Butts again, a very special friend whom I hadn't seen for several years. We talked about my recent divorce, Cyril and Nick, but avoided mentioning guinea pigs, spiny mice, gerbils and deer mice. She told me that she and Roger were considering divorce too. It was as catching as calicivirus.

Don't look a gift-donkey in the mouth was my new motto, and when Jenny came to Cott to tea one Sunday afternoon, every cloud in the sky had a silver lining. I was in the kitchen looking out of the window to where she was sitting on the lawn. I saw an attractive woman with short blonde hair, wearing a pretty floral-patterned summer dress, sitting on the lawn near the bridge over the stream. Uncanny, unnerving, but comforting.

She told me she and her cousin, when they were young, often talked of their ideal home… a cottage in the country with an orchard; a stream at the bottom of the garden, and a donkey in the field. While it was too early to say that love was blossoming, buds were definitely budding.

At the end of the French Revolution, the poet William Wordsworth wrote:

'Bliss was it in that Dawn to be alive, but to be young was very heaven.'

I was alive, nearly young, and in seventh heaven.

*

While my first marriage was not something I entered into lightly, a second one needed thought, planning and courage. Deep in thought, planning and courage, I was forced back to the real world by a phone call from Brian Arthur, the Director for Leisure and Tourism for Restormel Council. Following many months of negotiating, which consisted of two presentations to the council; four sub-council meetings, and many discussions with Brian Arthur, he informed me that I was to be the new owner of Cornwall Animal World.

Months earlier, when my accountant heard I was hoping to buy a zoo, he said, 'I've never heard of anyone buying a zoo before, especially a failing one. Anyone doing that would have to be bloody mad.' That's when I thought of Roger Martin. We had been friends for many years, which was surprising since I almost got him shot... twice.

The first time was at a cricket match in Devon where we were both playing. During the tea break we were talking together on the balcony of the clubhouse when a bullet thudded into the wall no more than six inches above his head. Sometimes it paid to be short. Someone had been shooting rabbits in a nearby field, and that day Roger and the rabbit had a lucky escape.

The second time, we both found ourselves in a situation of great danger. A friend had invented heat packs using waste materials – rectangular blocks of a mixture of saw dust, waste engine oil and waste molasses to increase heat and create a pleasant smell, all of which was bonded together by a coating of cement. He needed help to market them, and asked me. I enlisted the help of my friend Roger, having told him that it was a product that would probably make us a lot of money. The mention of money worked every time.

We went to the Egyptian Embassy in London where we were to demonstrate the qualities of the packs as a cheap heat source. The officers at the embassy didn't have a fireplace, but took us into a side street outside, which seemed an ideal place for our demonstration. I lit four of the rectangular blocks, which I had placed in a pile on top of each other to look like a mound of coal. Presentation is important. Flames and smoke leapt ten feet in the air, and the heat was intense. It was a success story which was about to have a sad ending when a policeman on a motorbike, siren blaring, appeared around the corner. Excitement at the success of our demonstration turned to fear as we watched him release what looked like a machine gun from its holder on the motor bike. It appeared that his finger was on the trigger, and he pointed the thing in our direction. He shot the blaze with his fire extinguisher. We were saved by the Egyptians, who explained why we had set fire to the street.

On the train home that evening Roger said, 'Never again.' However, never again was but temporary, because he was soon to become part-owner of Cornwall Animal World Ltd. When I told him it would make us a lot of money, he was for it. It never failed.

He, like me, was anxiously waiting for the OK signal from Restormel, so we were ready when I took the call. 'Congratulations Mike, you now own the lease of Cornwall Animal World.'

'Thanks Arthur.'

'My name's Brian.'

'Why is it called Animal World, Brian?'

'Because people don't like zoos.'

'They like animal worlds, do they?'

There was a long pause before he said, 'I'll speak to you about it when you come in to sign the contract. A letter is on its way.'

''Bye Brian.'

Councils are non-committal until they've had a meeting and taken a vote, so he'd need to ask the councillors about zoos becoming animal worlds. I joined Jenny, told her the news about my future employment, and enjoyed the afternoon in the company of my renewed friend.

A few days later when I talked to my new co-director, he wanted to know why it was called Animal World. I said that Brian Arthur was going to ask the council, but he thought it was because people didn't like zoos. 'Do they like animal worlds then?' he asked. Here we go again.

'Roger, let's call it Newquay Zoo like it used to be in the old days.'

So, Newquay Zoo was reborn, or, as Mike Pulley, our new bank manager put it, 'The phoenix will rise from the ashes.' Some phoenix. Some ashes. Some zoo.

I took my money out of the bank to buy the lease, which put me in the position of being without a bob or two again, financially insecure, but happy.

*

I started my new career on Good Friday, 1 April 1994, in heavy drizzle.

Our route to future prosperity was a simple one, since the Easter holiday is a busy time in Cornwall, especially in Newquay, and generally lasts for two weeks. Money would come rolling in I told Roger. He liked that.

We had advertised the Zoo as a popular visitor attraction for young and old and, full of hope, excitement and expectation, we commissioned a free bus service to transport people from the centre of town to the Zoo. We also advertised on commercial radio, and employed extra staff to cope with the rush. The shop was only a small kiosk, but we would make it bigger after Easter when the bank balance balanced better.

The staff looked smart in new uniforms, and the animal enclosures, old existing cages, toilets and grounds all had a facelift in time for the momentous occasion. The higher-than-anticipated overdraft would soon be a thing of the past, because hotels, guest houses and campsites were full.

By lunchtime on that first Good Friday only four holidaymakers had paid to come into the Zoo, and they were very wet. The drizzle had become real rain, and got heavier as the day progressed. By three o'clock gales drove the rain in through gaps in the office roof; through holes in the roof of the toilets, and through the badly fitted windows of the café. The Zoo was awash, and the deserted car-park was flooded. Waterproofed, I walked around my empire looking for the animals. I didn't see any.

Where were the lions... the pumas... the camels... the antelopes... the monkeys? Even the penguins were sheltering. The only people I saw were those who were paid to be there.

Geoff Gerry had been employed at the Zoo, née Animal World, for many years as the security guard. He stood in his sentry box and made sure that people who came in paid for admission. He was dry, there were no leaks in his sentry box. Geoff was a tall, substantial man of military

Geoff Gerry in his sentry box wearing the old uniform.

bearing, and wore what looked like a prison-warder's uniform, that was until I issued him with a new one, which was less intimidating to anyone who cared to join us for a day at the Zoo. He said he'd never seen a Good Friday as bad as this one. Ten visitors came that day, and Geoff, ever an optimist, said, 'There's always tomorrow.'

When tomorrow came it was worse, and flooding in the Zoo was a possibility. So were the next seven days. Where was Noah when he was needed? Geoff had definitely never seen anything like it, and the ark was in danger of sinking. Time to send out the doves!

But we owned a zoo. Not many people can say that.

During Easter, 208 visitors came to our zoo, and our total income was £1,456. Our expenditure was £7,300, which put us in a severe deficit situation. Brian Arthur dropped in, and said he'd never known an Easter like it.

We bought the lease on favourable terms because, as a business, it was in financial trouble. Over Easter nothing had changed. It had been losing money for several years and, due to lack of income, there had been lack of investment. Being council-owned it was the ratepayers who suffered the loss, and they, understandably, didn't like it. The only way it could succeed was in private ownership, with private investment. That Easter Roger and I suffered the loss instead, and we didn't like it either.

Geoff said that when the Zoo first opened in 1969 it was Newquay's jewel in the crown, but it had since become tarnished. Mike Pulley, our bank manager, wondered if the phoenix could rise from the ashes of such a dismal Easter holiday. He said he'd seen it all before.

My damp spirits dried as they basked in the warmth of the tail end of an April sun, and I hoped the phoenix could. After all, we owned a zoo. Not many can say that.

During the first staff meeting, attended by six keepers, four ladies in the café, Geoff, the receptionist who doubled as shop staff, and a part-time cleaner/driver, I outlined our future plans 'to get the Zoo back on its feet.'

A delegated spokesperson, who happened to be the cleaner/driver, told me in no uncertain terms that it was better when it was Cornwall Animal World; better in the ownership of Restormel Council, and I'd better watch my step, because the staff would complain to the union if I tried to make changes. Although there weren't many staff, those that there were indicated that they were happier without me, and were not prepared to comply with any of my requests, however reasonable.

I pressed on with my requests though:

1. *'I'd rather you didn't use the company phone, in the company time, to ring the betting shop to place bets on horses.'*

Amazement and innocence shone around. 'Who, me?'

2. To the lady cleaner/driver: *'Will you please clean the windows of the café.'*

To which she replied, 'The union will not allow me to climb a ladder, especially with no one holding it.' She only had to climb two rungs to reach the top of the window.

3. To the ladies in the café: *'I would be obliged if you would allow children to sit in the café with their parents.'*

The reply was, 'They make too much noise, so they must stay outside.'

4. *'I would like it if you would work five days per week on a rota system, which may mean weekend work.'*

Reply, 'We only intend to work five days per week, Monday to Friday. Usually only one person has to work on a weekend, and then it's paid at double time, it's union rules.'

I understood now why Animal World had been costing the taxpayers so much money, and had been in danger of bankruptcy.

However, this was a zoo; we were dealing with living creatures which did not recognize Monday-to-Friday rules.

The staff had worked within the comfort rules of the council and the union for too long, and changes were about to take place. Of the thirteen staff employed, seven resigned.

*

Since we needed to look after our animals and our visitors, it was important to become a profitable business. To be 'a jewel in Newquay's crown' needed commitment, not needless confrontation or union interference. In order to make the jewel sparkle I needed staff I could rely on. The six who stayed became loyal, good friends, hard-working and committed. Three of them in particular I could never have managed without. Commitm? works both ways.

Cheski with a lemur.

Geoff, the security guard in the days of Cornwall Animal World, knew the Zoo from its beginning in 1969, and was a respected resident of Newquay, invaluable in our work with the community. Mark Tomaczeski (Cheski) was a quiet guy, dedicated to his work as a keeper of primates and big cats. He was tall, thin, and arrived for work every day clean-shaven, but by late afternoon the five-o'clock-shadow crept slowly over much of his face; a beard would have suited him. Pete Trebilcock had worked as a keeper for many years before I arrived, and was a mine of information regarding the functioning of the Zoo. He was destined to become my operations manager later on, liaising between keeping staff, all other facilities, and customer care. A manager of any business is only as good as his staff. I was lucky.

Although in the early days finance was a problem and wages were poor, I tried to make up for the shortcoming in other ways. There would be no organized break times, but chatting to visitors was an essential part of staff duties, often over a coffee on the patio, and had no time limit. If anyone got into financial difficulty, or needed help in any way, talk to the management – i.e., me. There would be no clocking in and out; it would be a matter of trust. We were all in this together, for better or worse. While we could not pay for overtime work, success for the company would result in bonuses and extra time off. It was not all about money, job satisfaction was important.

Our Easter profits had not materialized; the bank balance didn't, and losses had increased. It became obvious that if substantial development did not happen the Zoo's current poor reputation might still result in bankruptcy. A further loan was required immediately.

Mike Pulley, a master of clichés, explained that we had 'a steep hill to climb'. He understood the precariousness of the tourist industry; the dependence on the weather for its success, and, so far, we had been unlucky. He said that if we were prepared to increase our financial risk he could offer a loan, so we gave all our insurance policies as securities; the deeds of Cott Farm, and the twenty-year lease of the Zoo. Albeit precariously, we were back in business.

That first year we intended to renew and extend pathways; plant exotic gardens; build a shop; remove antiquated cages; renovate enclosures; redesign the café; build a new entrance; renew the toilets; include ▪bled facilities; repair the roof in my office, and create new signs. Considerable development in a short time, and at considerable expense, Mike reminded us.

The building site that the Zoo then became was not conducive to holiday entertainment, but it did attract the curious. 'I wonder what's happening there?'

*

But I had other things on my mind. Jenny's divorce was finalized. We went to the Highbullen Hotel in North Devon for a weekend holiday. I was a frequent visitor to this delightful hotel in Chittlehamholt, and became friends with the owners, a wonderful eccentric couple, Hugh and Pam Neil. They invited us to have lunch with them and their family before we were due to leave three days later.

While we were in North Devon we visited two other zoos, Combe Martin and Exmoor, to look at ideas that might be useful to Newquay Zoo. Piracy was commonplace in our industry. There was a great brotherhood, because care of animals is of paramount importance, and it was not a case of 'pinching' ideas, so much as 'exchanging' them. Over the years I made many friends, and exchanged many ideas.

However, our few days' break in Devon became a literal reality when, before lunch with the Neils, I fell and damaged my ankle playing table tennis. Hugh was of the opinion that liberal doses of brandy would ease the pain. He must have felt my pain too, because between us we finished the whole bottle. By the time Jenny and I arrived at the Accident and Emergency department at Treliske Hospital in Truro on Sunday evening I was painless and legless.

'Have you been skiing ?' the doctor asked when he examined my definitely broken ankle.

'No, playing table tennis!' Apparently skiing was a much more popular way of breaking ankles.

'We don't get many broken ankles from table-tennis players.'

For the next seven weeks Jenny and a wheelchair provided my care and mobility. The new Noah's Ark entrance was underway; the café and patio were completed; the shop was almost built; toilets were renovated; my office roof no longer leaked; new paths had been laid; redundant cages had been removed, and existing ones renovated. There was even enough money left to create island enclosures on a couple of the lakes.

One of the best and most visual transformations had been made by Exotic Clive. Clive Shilton, the owner of Hardy Exotics Nursery near Penzance, hadn't always been a horticulturist. He used to be a cobbler, and made the shoes for Princess Diana for her marriage to Prince Charles. He was about to make nature's wedding dress for Newquay Zoo, and he started with a jungle. It was only a little one, but as Clive said, 'It'll be a big one in five years' time.'

I couldn't wait, I wanted it straight away. He gave in to my wishes by planting four large tree ferns, some gunnera, and a banana plant with one banana on it. Gunnera look like giant rhubarb leaves. It made me feel better to see real trees and big rhubarb leaves. Jungles don't happen

The café and patio.

overnight, but the Zoo looked more like one by the time our new loan was almost exhausted and the plaster cast was removed from my leg.

We were still lacking enough of the 'Wonder-what's-happening-there' people to make a profit, and, what made things more difficult was that I broke my ankle again. This time switching off the television. I didn't dare tell the doctor how I'd done it. I can't think they get many broken ankles from switching off televisions.

Then we ran out of money.

However, we were 'thrown a lifeline' by our bank manager, who, in view of the progress made, sympathy for my broken ankle, and our 'undoubted enthusiasm,' as he put it, offered to add another £100,000 to the loan, for only 'a little collateral'. Little was a lot. In fact, it was all we had, but lifelines only save you when you grab them.

Bad News

A phone call at the Zoo early one morning was from my brother. My mother had been taken ill and was in hospital. This was difficult to take in; she was seventy-six, and had always been so fit, well and active. At the age of sixty-three she passed five O-level exams. After my father died, she decided to learn to drive and, five attempts later, at the age of sixty-nine, she passed. She also belonged to a dancing club and a swimming club, and her ambition was to walk the path of Offa's Dyke with me. Offa's Dyke stretched from Shropshire to Monmouthshire. A long walk.

Shortly after she passed her driving test, I went to visit her. She drove the car through the open doors of the timber garage and straight out the other side. Her foot had slipped off the brake on to the accelerator. Between us, we lifted the splintered wooden wall of the garage off the badly dented car. My mother surveyed the damage and said, 'Well, I've never done that before. I'd better go and make us some tea.'

Now she was very ill.

Since my ankle was back in plaster, one of my staff drove me to the hospital in Newport, a journey of four hours. Being so far away and immersed in my own affairs, I had not always been the diligent son. It had taken her illness to make me realize it, and seeing her now in a hospital bed, looking frail, breathing with difficulty, I was filled with regret at my lack of attention. She didn't like loneliness, nor did she like getting old, and faced it with some trepidation. She had always done so much for her family, and had been there for me when I was an adult having adult problems. She was there for Jan and me when Ami died, and understood the sadness of our loss. Ben and Holly were my step-children and they were her step-grandchildren. She was proud of this, and loved being their step-granny.

Now, in the hospital, I was looking at the lady who had looked after us when we were sick; made us laugh when we were sad, and had worked all her life to make our lives happy and successful. Although almost three hundred miles away, with a struggling business and a broken ankle, I visited her at least twice a week. My brother Richard and sister Sue, who both lived in Wales with their families, visited every day, and took turns in being with her at night. Despite her pain and discomfort she smiled, chatted and remained cheerful. I remember her looking out of her hospital bedroom window on the fourth floor, seeing the sun and blue sky, and asking 'Will you take me outside? I need to be in the fresh air.' She was an outside person. It wasn't possible, but I said we would go outside on my next visit when she was better.

There were often times during the next six weeks, when Jenny came with me to see her, but she wasn't well enough to be taken out into the blue sky and fresh air. On one of our visits she took hold of Jenny's hand. 'If anything happens to me before you marry Michael, I'd like you to wear my wedding ring.' We didn't think anything was going to happen to her for a long time, nor had we made wedding plans, but we said we'd see her at the wedding. She turned to me and said, 'If you are going to get married, you'd better get a new jacket.'

When we arrived at the hospital the next morning, I was wearing a new green jacket. We drove back to Cornwall promising to see her in a week's time, and take her into the sun and fresh air. My brother phoned me that evening to say that Mam was fine; she'd told him that Jenny and I were getting married, and that she was looking forward to being at the wedding.

Those who visited in the next few months were made welcome by a large number of staff with little to do. I overheard one visitor say, 'Coming to this zoo gets us away from the crowds in Newquay.' Another was heard to say, 'What a lovely little zoo this is, and there are no crowds.'

But we needed the crowds. The season ended just as it started: wet with few visitors, and prompted Geoff to say it was worse than last year. Downcast and a little downhearted, we wondered if Brian Arthur had been right. Perhaps people didn't like zoos. Was owning a zoo such a good idea after all?

Negative thoughts were not to be encouraged. Lateral thinking, new ideas and new developments were needed if Newquay Zoo was to succeed, and with money running out again this was far from easy. We had intended to remain open all year, but now wondered at the wisdom of such a decision. Brian Arthur didn't think it was a good idea, telling us that the council used to close in September, just like most attractions did, since it was not profitable to be open. However, we stayed open, and hoped things would change. Just because it was winter Cornwall was not closed. I belonged to the school of thought that believed 'considered risk-taking' was important for success.

Early in October a coach drove into the car-park carrying a group of children from a special school, and their accompanying staff. 'Is the Zoo open? Nowhere else is.' Some of the children were in wheelchairs; some were blind, and others were mentally handicapped. During their stay, they held snakes, tortoises, rabbits and hedgehogs; they laughed, clapped their hands when they heard the lions roaring, and loved the feeding times for the penguins and raccoons. Cheski, the keeper in charge of primates, took some of the children on to the island to help feed the lemurs.

A week later a letter arrived from the head of the school saying that the children arrived home tired but excited. They still talked about their visit to Newquay Zoo, and wanted to come again.

A newborn hedgehog.

Nursing a baby raccoon.

Cornwall was open. Three more coaches arrived during the next couple of weeks. Two of them brought groups of disabled children, while the third carried a group of elderly people. Seeing the enjoyment and happiness that being with the animals gave them was enough to convince us that people do like zoos, especially ours.

We owned a zoo, and not many can say that.

The Strong Wind of Change

22 October 1994 was the day I got married again. Ben drove us from Cott Farm to the registry office in his yellow Vauxhall Astra, which he decorated with balloons and white ribbons. Gale-force winds and rain accompanied us to the registry office, and by the time we arrived the balloons and ribbons had blown away.

I wore the green jacket my mother bought me, and Jenny wore a red jacket. We looked like a couple of traffic lights, but despite the rain, our colourful rainbow was an arc of sunshine. Jenny's parents, Cecil and Doreen, were there; so was her aunt Greta, several of her friends, and her ex-parents-in-law, Jean and Bob. I'd met them all at Jenny's first wedding, and little had changed, except we were all older. Those who had not been at Jenny's first wedding were her daughter Jo, Ben, my brother and his wife, my sister and her husband, and several of my friends. My mother's wedding ring fitted perfectly. Memories would never die.

After the ceremony we had a blessing at Gunwalloe, in a small church on the beach on the Lizard Peninsula. The Revd Peter Long, a good friend, officiated. He not only officiated, but helped me direct cars into the church car-park. From a distance it must have been a strange sight – two men, one in what looked like a white dress, the other in a bright green jacket, both of them waving their arms on a windswept beach.

Although the gales blew us into the church, the sun peered out somewhat nervously through the clouds, and shone on us as we came out. The bride and groom were greeted with a confetti of soapy bubbles blown by the guests and the wind. Our reception was held at a bistro on the Trelowarren estate, where I welcomed everyone and said how delighted I was to see so many friends and relations again who had been at Jenny's last wedding. I said how pleased I was to see those who were here for the first time. It was inevitable that my speech should refer to the guinea pigs, gerbils, spiny mice and deer mice, and everyone who knew of the massacre was pleased to hear that the sole survivor, a deer mouse, eventually died of old age.

Mike Scott, my Best Man, told the guests that the first time he met Jenny was at Cott Farm, when he thought she was the young lady from Meals on Wheels bringing me my lunch. A week later, my Meals-on-Wheels lady and I went to the Maldives for our honeymoon, where, among the rocks, gether, in return for adoption of an animal and free entry for their staff. A couple of companies even offered money as sponsorship. Desperation became less desperate; no one had the stomach for having to put down animals, and I could not have asked for more loyalty when my staff volunteered to work extra hours for no extra pay.

We had no more collateral to offer as security, other than obtaining a longer lease, which, indeed, was a high-risk strategy, and not to be entered into lightly. The lease was personal to Roger and me, and did not end with insolvency. The buck stopped with us. The consequences of failure would be dire.

However, when the council agreed to the extension, we were able to look upward and onward. With more collateral to offer, and the faith of companies that agreed to support us, the bank increased facilities once more. With the help of friends of the Zoo, we secured a council grant, a development grant, and an extra loan guaranteed by the Department of Trade and Industry (DTI).

*

Jon Blount, who thought he'd be 'on his bike' by now, was delighted at the prospect of further development opportunities. Staff jobs were safe, and we were entering a time of excitement and enthusiasm.

Our recently formed marketing group was also full of excitement and enthusiasm. Collectively we could now promote Trenance Gardens as an exciting tourism venue offering diverse, quality attractions. Waterworld, a swimming and fitness complex, is located at the end of the large car-park; John Littlefield owned The Crazy Golf Garden opposite the Zoo; Eric Booth, who owns Lappa Valley Steam Railway, also ran a delightful train ride in the Gardens; Geoff Warmington operated the Road Train from Newquay town centre to Trenance, and the Zoo was about to expand and develop.

We were all in good spirits by Christmas when the Revd Peter Long held our first Animals' Christmas Carol Service on a cold December afternoon. The early darkness was illuminated by lanterns and lights on a Christmas tree on the patio overlooking the lake. Makeshift enclosures, made from hay bales, provided stalls for a llama, a sheep, two pigs and a goat, which, during 'Away in a Manger', happily munched their way through the tasty enclosures, and the Revd Peter Long's notes, which he had dropped.

Animals, staff and visitors celebrated a traditional Christmas. The festive season had come to the Zoo. Geoff squeezed into a Father Christmas outfit two sizes too small for him and gave out presents, while Mark Norris, still teaching but on holiday, entertained visitors with his animal puppet show. The Zoo grounds and the animal enclosures had been festively decorated with suitable greenery, which the monkeys ate while visitors ate mince pies and drank hot punch. Brian Arthur brought the Mayor of Restormel to wish everyone a happy Christmas. Seeing so many visitors he said, 'It seems that people do like zoos after all.'

They certainly liked ours, and on New Year's Day, staff and visitors toasted the rebirth of Newquay Zoo with glasses of champagne.

*

Owning a zoo was about caring for animals and people. In Victorian and Edwardian times zoos did just that, but the animals were in cages, which is no longer considered to be the best practice. Even so, it was probably done with the best of intentions. In those days, people couldn't visit far-off lands to see, smell and hear exotic animals, so the animals were brought to the people, who dressed up for a visit to the zoological garden – a place of beauty, of shrubs, trees and flowers with wonderful smells, and animals from far-away places. It was a place of wonderment, excitement and discovery.

It was these early zoological gardens that raised an awareness of the need to look after animals and our environment. As forerunners of modern zoo-practice and the scientific research now undertaken, they offered enlightenment, entertainment and consideration. Progress makes perfection, a goal to be aimed for. If it wasn't for the early zoos many species of animals would be extinct.

Running one today is not dissimilar to running a hospital, a restaurant and a hotel... all three that is. Meticulous records of births, injuries, illnesses and medications are kept on computers or in files, or preferably, both. Bloodlines and parentage are circulated to zoos world-wide to enable breeding programmes to be undertaken, and deaths are notified to stud-book keepers, who control the breeding of endangered species, and determine animal pairings. They are the registrars of births, marriages and deaths of the animal kingdom.

When diseases occur, especially if contagious, detailed documentation is circulated to zoos, wildlife parks and veterinary establishments worldwide, in order to contain and, hopefully, cure. Food, diets and medications are prepared and weighed, to ensure that animals receive the correct balance of proteins, carbohydrates and vitamins. Hygiene, disposal of waste, and cleaning, are high priorities.

For the animals, living in a well-run zoo is like being in a five-star hotel, where good food, comfortable accommodation, good facilities, room-service, free medical care and entertainment are provided. We were part of this organization, and were aiming for five-star grading.

When we bought the lease, Cornwall Animal World didn't have one star, but, by the time our second anniversary arrived, although we had not had many visitors, a great deal of development had been undertaken, and the Zoo looked all of three-star standard. Two more to go.

*

A newly constructed enclosure became home to various species of bats, kinkajous and other nocturnal creatures, and infra-red lights enabled

Lechwe antelope on the African Plains (above and below). Porcupine (bottom).

legend says that God made tapirs out of all the bits left over when he had made the other animals.

The Tropical House became a walk-through rainforest experience, where birds, iguanas, pygmy marmosets, two sloths and two mouse deer lived. Climbing platforms were erected in the lions' enclosure, since for them, being constantly at ground level was far from stimulating.

Although there were still financial constraints, and pay-back time was fast approaching, it was exhilarating to see so much development. A new zoo had been born; the phoenix was rising from the ashes.

A paddock in the middle of the Zoo became the African Plains, and a couple of 'hills', complete with burrows and heating, had been made for a group of meerkats. They shared the paddock with porcupines and Lechwe antelopes, which enjoyed the boggy area we had created. To complete this enclosure of mixed species, we introduced Etosha, our elderly zebra.

Zebra on the African Plains (above). Sloth (below).

Etosha came to Newquay to retire, having been rejected by her 'herd' at another zoo. Zebras are not solitary animals, so the company of others was desirable. To move her from her existing paddock, where she was alone, was a difficult undertaking, which would normally require anaesthetizing her. This would have been dangerous at her age.

The greatest temptation for any animal is food. At the end of the day, when the Zoo was empty of visitors, keepers with large wooden panels made a wide tunnel from her paddock to the new plains enclosure. The journey of about a hundred yards had been rehearsed, and any possible difficulties prepared for. The lions – prone to roaring at evening time – had been shut into their indoor area and given extra food to keep them quiet. Zebras, being nutritious meals for hungry lions, get nervous when near them.

Gentle lemur.

ing the rewards of his work as they moved from bush to bush and plant to plant, without eating so much as a mouthful. Zoo horticulture became an important part of our work.

All animals in the wild live in nature's environment... plants, shrubs, bushes and trees... a source of cover and food. Many animals, being vegetarians, rely on nature's environment for food, and all of them rely on nature's environment when they are unwell, since plants and herbs provide medication to cure many ailments.

Such herbal remedies are natural medicines for humans as well. At the Zoo we set aside a large area in which our gardener, Mike Perry, assisted by Les Beckett in the maintenance department, planted and nurtured many species of herbs to treat minor animal ailments. While some herbs were administered as part of the feeding regime, we attached 'window boxes' planted with herbs to the bars of the Diana monkeys, Colobus and Mangabeys' cages. Over a period of months we observed and recorded which herbs were most popularly used by these monkeys.

It was useful to find out the eating habits of many of our wild animals, and to consider whether herbs provided remedies and safeguards against ailments. Birds, animals and people find cures from nature's rich environment.

Good zoos provide research and a wealth of discovery for visitors. Our visitors enjoyed our 'ever-changing zoo'. Animals were born; animals arrived from other zoos; animals left to go to other zoos, and new enclosures were built.

*

The hardest part of a zoo-keeper's life is the death of an animal. Chunky, the Zoo's last surviving brown bear, was ill. He was old, blind, and had been diagnosed with liver cancer. During the early days of our ownership someone had complained to the local newspaper because he was living alone 'in a concrete bear pit'. Bears are solitary animals in the wild, but, in a zoo, companionship is desirable. At his age however, and in his state of health, the introduction of another animal would have led to fighting, or at the very least caused stress. Animals often reject others which are not fit and well. We were fully aware of the inadequacies of his enclosure, and would not have wished to bring other bears into it anyway, but being blind, Chunky knew his way around his concrete home, and to have altered it would have confused him. To us it was inadequate, but to Chunky it was his home, where he felt secure. Security is as necessary for animals as it is for people.

Being unwell, he no longer took exercise, preferring to sleep and rest inside his den. He was not eating, not even the fish that Cheski daily held out for him. Old age had crept up on him, and it was terminal. Had it been otherwise, we would not have contemplated euthanasia.

The vet's injection took effect, and Chunky died peacefully.

When death occurs in a zoo, whether naturally, or by euthanasing, sadness is felt by everyone. We were all sad when Chunky died, even though he had gone to another place where he was at peace, and his spirit was free. For Cheski, still holding the fish, he had not just lost one of his animals, he had lost a friend. As he walked away I saw his tears.

A few days after Chunky's death, a letter arrived addressed to me. It was from a lady who visited the Zoo practically every day, and had done so for many years. It was her sanctuary, where she found peace in the company of animals, and her favourite animal was Chunky. She accused me of killing him, 'a decision you made purely for financial reasons,' she said. Although her reaction was understandable, there was no truth in such an accusation, for had there been any chance of Chunky getting better, money would have been made available, regardless of the cost. Some days later she arrived at my office with two Restormel Council officers. One of them was Brian Arthur.

Despite my explanation of Chunky's condition, and the reason for euthanasing, her opinion of me did not alter. She wasn't prepared to accept that this was a welfare issue; that a decision had been made in the interests of the animal. 'Who are you to make such a decision? You are not God.'

Being the owner of a zoo at that moment was not the best job in the world, and I could see that Restormel's officers agreed with me. I didn't see her again for several weeks. Eventually, she returned, avoiding me, quickening her steps in the opposite direction when I approached. The Zoo was still her sanctuary, preferably without me.

The intensity of her feelings was uncomfortable, but I hoped that one day she would understand my action, because it was my responsibility to make decisions which were in the interests of the animals, not people. Hopefully, I would see her in better times.

Upset, but undeterred by this character assassination, I had other work to attend to in the Zoo. Diana monkeys needed me.

Barley the sheep.

Mark Norris had left his teaching job at Mullion School to join the permanent staff as Education Officer, and a bachelor group of four Sulawesi crested macaques arrived from Jersey Zoo to take up residence in Chunky's converted home.

The first visitors to the newly arrived monkeys were a group of ladies from the local Women's Institute, who were delighted to see them mating. One lady said, 'It just shows how contented they are.' When I explained that they were all males, and that the females would arrive shortly, she was not deterred, 'Never mind, I expect they're practising,' she said.

Practice makes perfect, and when the girls arrived the guys were ready to meet them. But introductions had to wait. The females were confined to an inner room for a time, where boys and girls could see, smell and hear each other. Togetherness was not allowed, in order to avoid any fighting that could occur. There was much waving of arms and gnashing of teeth (or was it smiling in anticipation?). After a week of confinement and deprivation, socializing began. A few minor skirmishes took place to establish their hierarchical positions, before the group settled down. Hemlock became the dominant leader, the alpha male whose job it was to keep law and order and maintain a routine.

Without the alpha male the group would be directionless. There would undoubtedly, sometime in the future, be challenges to his leadership from other males, especially if he showed signs of weakness. However, for now, the black apes prospered, and so did we.

While our income was improving, having pulled back from the edge of bankruptcy, we were still a long way from the comfort zone. We tried many ways to increase income. In the summer we stayed open during the evenings, which proved not to be a wise move. It increased our expenditure, but the income from so few visitors was insufficient to cover costs. Childrens' birthday parties achieved a modicum of success, and selling yearly season tickets, with discounted admission charges, we hoped would help our cash flow. But this too was almost abandoned, until we met Rosalie Cooper.

Rosalie had almost decided, but not quite, that a season ticket would make an ideal present for her husband's birthday. After a great deal of deliberation, and a little persuasion from Geoff, she did decide, although she was worried that Norman might not like the Zoo as much as she did. Norman became our first season-ticket holder, and it was the start of a wonderful friendship. It was also the start of a successful season-ticket membership, where all who joined became Friends of the Zoo.

*

My twice-daily inspection revealed an emerging jungle and rainforest. Clive had been right, the Zoo was growing up. Our accountant gave an encouraging report of the financial situation when he said that the third year's loss was likely to be less than the second year's loss, which had been less than the first year's loss.

I saw the bank manager's eyes glaze over at that point. For those financially inclined, our first year's loss was £196,000, which our accountant said meant that we were technically insolvent. By the end of the second year, the loss had been reduced to £71,000, and this was almost as good as making a profit, he said. Who was he kidding?

Mike Pulley had now got to grips with the good news, so when the meeting ended I took him on a tour of the Zoo. He was impressed with the jungle, 'I'm glad to see the bank's money is growing,' he said.

Hopefully, the work of the gardener, Mike Perry, in the overgrown and neglected Oriental Garden, would help it to grow further. He had planted bamboos, acers and maple trees, as well as flowering shrubs. In this haven of tranquillity, we built a house for our Asian short-clawed otters. An area of stream and pond was staked out as their enclosure, which led on to a sand and rock Japanese garden via a short pathway. To one side of this we built aviaries holding cockatoos and love birds. A pebble path led to a

Asian short-clawed otter.

raised platform on which sat a stone statue of Buddha, who, as the centre-piece looking down on the visitors, was the focal point in the garden.

As well as creating more interest in the Zoo grounds, and offering a quiet place to sit and reflect, the Oriental Garden became a facility for schools to study comparative religions. They often held costumed processions through the grounds, with music, dance and storytelling, ending at the 'Buddha Shrine'.

This practical, 'hands-on' education was an ideal learning process. But not everyone agreed, as this letter from a local resident, which followed a warning I had received a few days earlier, demonstrated.

13/08/96

Dear Mr Thomas,
Curse of Buddhist Shrine.
I appreciate that you are not a Christian believer or you would never have allowed a Buddhist shrine at the Zoo. Obviously, if you had any fear of God you would have taken "my previous warning" seriously. Since you do not, like any prophecy of God, the word had been spoken and you have witnessed it. Unless there is repentance, at some time in the future, it may be many years from now, when God chooses to act, you and all who have knowledge of this letter will know that God is a just God.

A passive acceptance of all and anything will never bring world peace. Truth cannot live beside a lie. All the time that there is good and evil, light and darkness there will be unrest, wars and hatred. It is the Devil that causes the problems in the world. If you do not accept the existence of a Devil, that will not make him cease to exist, any more than if you denied the existence of America. The Lord Jesus clearly teaches:- "Love your enemies". It must be seen then, that any war in the name of Christianity, has the devil's signature.

Christianity will never share a bed with other religions. Only in the Christian faith is the forgiveness of sins found. Only the blood of the Lord Jesus Christ has the power to wash a sinner clean.

You said Britain's heritage was pagan and that you were helping to make it multicultural. What you are saying is, that Britain was pagan and you want it to be pagan again. Have you no comprehension of the hundreds of thousands of Christian martyrs who gave their lives, often being tortured to death, to make Britain a free Christian nation? While the tide of apathy and deception has washed our shores over the last 70 years, our land is still enjoying the fruit of the lives of our God fearing forefathers.

God will not ignore your Buddhist Shrine, but he is full of mercy and forgiveness. I would urge you to reconsider your actions, and never give up in your quest for the truth. Jesus said, "Seek and you shall find". If you ask the Lord to reveal himself to you he will.

I would like to make it quite clear that this "letter" is a response to a genuine concern.

I have included the letter in its entirety in order to question how anyone could be so didactic and not want to understand other points of view. There are many religions in our world, why should only one be the right one? Such an attitude has been responsible for creating many wars and devastation over the years. I had been warned that I was in danger of suffering God's wrath, which surely is not what religion is about, whatever form of worship is practised. In the wrong hands, religion can be a dangerous tool.

The practices taught by Buddha are timeless and universally applicable, and may well help give answers to questions that cannot be found elsewhere. Through the teachings of Buddha, 'the wheels of Dharma', we may protect ourselves from suffering and problems. This may be the means by which we can improve the quality of our lives, helping us to find inner peace and happiness. I don't regret creating such an awareness; in fact, I see it as being my responsibility.

P... P... P... Pick Up a Penguin

Having been hand-reared when his mother rejected him at birth, Peru was a superior bird, streetwise, smart, and the foreman of the flock. At feeding times, twice a day, he took his position at the gate inside the enclosure, watching for the approaching meal, ready to give the signal to the others.

He was not only the foreman but the lead-singer of the ten-strong, unmelodic choir of penguins that heralded the coming of buckets of sprats. Squawks and groans, pitched somewhere between baritone and first bass, with an occasional second tenor joining in for harmony, was their way of welcoming sprats. Peru, however, stood well apart from the others, waiting for me to talk to the visitors at the poolside.

The keeper threw fish into the pool, while nine hungry penguins dived and swam gracefully, hurtling after their elusive meal. An underwater ballet was in motion. But Peru was not for dancing, he waited for me to drop fish into his ever-open, upward-pointing beak.

Penguins can tilt their heads upwards and backwards without overbalancing, which is far from easy, and a good trick if you can do it, but it helped me to find his mouth without coming into contact with a sharp beak.

We had called Peru 'he' for several years before discovering that he was really 'she'. Birds are not easy to sex, and our discovery was only made by a scientific analysis of one of the feathers... DNA! So, at the end of feeding time, a lady waited for me to open the gate for her daily walk. A penguin of habit, she walked towards the lion enclosure, where the roars and smell of these large, four-legged beasts didn't frighten her at all. She was not part of their natural diet, unlike our free-ranging wallabies and mara, which avoided passing the lion enclosure at all costs.

A mara meets a peacock.

Her daily stroll was accompanied by visitors, and she led them past the black apes' enclosure to the Tropical House, which, for her, was a walk far enough. There she sat, waiting to be picked up and carried back, amid applause from appreciative visitors.

It was after one of the talks and walks, having carried Peru into the enclosure, that I joined Mike Kent sitting at a table on the lawn at Tippy's Snack Bar. The snack bar used to be an enclosure for mongooses, but when our mongooses wandered too far, being wanderlusts with a taste for adventure, Jenny suggested that it might be best to relocate their wandering to another zoo, and make their enclosure into an exotic snack bar – a profit centre which, in its early days, was run by my daughter Holly and her husband Dave.

Tippy's was so-named because it was adjacent to the enclosure where our male tapir lived with his mate Pepita and their new baby. A baby tapir is not at all like the adults, which have chocolate-brown, hairy skins. It is a little stripy creature, and looks just like a giant version of the mint humbugs that my gran used to give me on Sundays at Siloam Chapel. Jenny said it looked more like a marrow. If you can imagine a cross between a marrow and one of my gran's mint humbugs, you'll know what our little tapir looked like.

*

Mike Kent was waiting for me. He was a senior lecturer at St Austell College, and both of us had an educational dream to fulfil. I had bought a lease from Restormel Council on three acres of land adjoining the Zoo

Stripy mint humbug.

where Mike and I wanted to build a college for environmental and zoo studies. Education had always been, and still is, important to me. Although we had the support of St Austell College through the determination of Mike Kent, there were many hurdles to overcome before the dream would become a reality. Mike was the co-ordinator of our efforts, and the driving force that would help it to happen.

This latest meeting would be yet another hurdle vaulted on our way to the winning post. We discussed the course content and curriculum prepared for Exeter and Plymouth Universities to consider validation, without which there would be no financial assistance and no recognition of professional courses. In fact, there would be no college. Without the validation, the building, which we had already designed, would be consigned to the bin. Mike and our Education Officer, Mark Norris, were going to make the presentation to the board in Plymouth.

A Loose Kneecap

It was while Mike and Mark were in Plymouth that Geoff, 'Zoo 14', issued a Gamma warning. Melanie, aged eleven, had run from the African Plains enclosure to tell him that one of the 'kneecaps' had dug his way out of the enclosure. 'Kneecaps' are social animals, and live in large colonies in Africa. Often, several of them can be seen sitting on their haunches looking skyward to warn others of approaching danger. In Newquay, their

Sentry duty.

only predators were seagulls, which sometimes 'dive-bombed' them, and had been seen to pick up babies and fly off with them in their beaks. Vigilance was required, even in the relative safety of the Zoo.

When Geoff and I arrived at the African Plains, Alonso was trying to dig his way back in. He'd found that the grass was not greener on the other side, and by chewing through the wire at the bottom of the enclosure fence he made it back to 'the family'. Meerkat numbers were restored. Before Melanie left that day, she was given a photograph of Alonso the 'kneecap'.

This reminded me of one of my early-morning walks around the Zoo when I was confronted with the whole gang of meerkats, having dug their way out of the enclosure, running down the path towards my office. Seeing me they stopped; sat on their haunches; looked in my direction; turned, and ran straight back into the enclosure. 'That's the power of being the boss,' Geoff said.

It was the year that the Mayor of Restormel held her Summer Charity Fête at the Zoo, and the year that Roger, my co-director, delivered some bad news which he and I discussed while we sat on the patio overlooking the squirrel monkeys' island. It was a peaceful scene, shattered by the news of his impending divorce. He had been married twice before, but, judging by his upset state, it didn't get any easier. I'd been to all his weddings, and thoroughly enjoyed them. Hoping it might cheer him up, I said how much I'd enjoyed them. But he left without eating his cake, or drinking his tea. It was not the time to eat and drink. A few days later he said he was going to Spain for a month on a walking holiday. A long walk would do him good.

Jenny and I didn't go to Spain, but we went to Jersey to meet Jeremy Mallinson, who had taken charge of Jersey Zoo on the death of its founder, Gerald Durrell. Jeremy had worked there for many years and, together with Dr Lee Durrell, Gerald's wife, continued the Zoo's mission statement in Gerald Durrell's name. Jersey Zoo was my role model, and I believed that if I got anywhere near its standard my goal would be achieved. We were getting close, but more ideas were needed.

Jeremy was one of the most delightful and professional people I have ever met, and during the time I knew him, much of the advice he gave me proved invaluable. Jersey Zoo had pioneered 'free-ranging' monkey species in UK zoos, and this was what I wanted to do. Jeremy was very patient when we walked around, since I stopped every few yards to write down what he said, not wanting to miss anything. One piece of advice stayed with me... 'In our business expect the unexpected and there will be no surprises.'

This was easier said than done. Our business never failed to surprise me, and some weeks later, when Jon Blount made an Alpha warning over the radio, I tried very hard not to be surprised.

It was early morning, and the Zoo was not yet open to the public.

An Alpha alert was the most serious warning... , and this was. Jon took charge. A black ape had swung up and over the hot wires at the top of the enclosure, and was heading, via the trees which Exotic Clive had planted, towards my office, from where the entrance gate would be easily climbed.

Black apes are incredibly strong and dangerous, especially when frightened, and would be capable of killing a person. This one had left the safety of the enclosure and the security of the group and, as far as it was concerned, was in great danger. An animal hurt, cornered or frightened is an aggressive animal, and will do whatever is necessary to protect itself. The curator and senior primate keeper armed themselves with a dart gun to tranquilize it, and a .22 rifle, which would only be used as a last resort if the ape should attempt to leave the Zoo or attack someone.

It was a tense time. Movement had to be kept to a minimum and, as luck would have it, the morning cleaner had left the door open leading to the ladies' toilet. To the ape it meant safety. When keepers following it banged loudly on metal trays to create as much noise as possible, the ape sought refuge there. Although still a dangerous situation, it was fascinating to watch the ape's behaviour, trying to hide rather than attack. Now wasn't the time for it to attack, it was time to get away from the noise.

The entrance gate was no longer the desired escape route, nor was my office... the ladies' toilet was the ideal hiding place. While the noises continued, the ape showed fear rather than aggression. The curator was at the ready with the dart gun, while other keepers secured a strong net across the doorway. When the net was firmly in place, more noises, now from behind the ape, outside the toilets, drove it straight into the net, where it became tangled, enabling Jon to fire the dart gun containing a

Little Venus didn't disappoint his dad.

quick-reacting tranquillizer, which took a couple of minutes to take effect while the ape's struggles decreased.

The sleeping ape was transferred to a transportation cage, and was still asleep on arrival in one of the 'dens'. Jon fired another dart, containing the reversal dose to awaken it, from the safety of a hatch in the closed door. Our sleeping beauty was none other than Hemlock, the alpha male.

The emergency procedure had been handled skilfully, and when Delta was called on the radio, meaning emergency over, it was a welcome signal, since it was time to open the Zoo to visitors. Hemlock, none the worse for his adventure, was soon up and about, but not before another couple of 'hot wires' had been added to the enclosure. Some months later, he became a proud and protective father. Little Venus did not disappoint his dad.

Animals don't 'escape' because they are unhappy; they do so out of curiosity. In good zoos, they would probably rather get in than out, since safety and a good supply of food are high on the list of their priorities. In the wild it is often difficult for animals to hunt in safety and, as more forests vanish, they become more exposed to danger while looking for food. Zoos offer safe havens, and in safe and secure havens animals are likely to breed.

Breeding is not always a zoo priority, especially for animals that are not endangered. However, the more destruction that takes place in the name of progress, the more animals will need our care and protection.

*

Lizzie.

African lions, not yet on the endangered species list, are declining rapidly in numbers because of an intrusion into their hunting territory for reclamation of land, irresponsible hunting, and the spread of diseases. Animals can catch diseases and illnesses from humans.

Our two lions are residents in Newquay Zoo's retirement home, and not part of a breeding programme. They are the symbols of the Zoo, and many visitors' favourite animals. It was a sad day when Ross died of old age. He and Lizzie had come to the Zoo sixteen years earlier, when Ross was three years old and fully grown. Lizzie, who had been born in a zoo, had not yet reached adulthood. Ross had been hand reared when his mother – also hand reared – died giving birth, and he'd had the freedom of the farmhouse where he was born until he was considered too wild and dangerous. Wildness in animals is an instinct, not a term to describe violent behaviour.

People kept lions as pets before the Dangerous Wild Animal Act of 1976 made it difficult to do so, but still today, with a licence, it is possible to keep wolves, big cats, reptiles and other exotic animals. The licence laws, however, are generally sufficiently strict to prevent cruelty, and routine inspections reveal any ill treatment.

A favourite story of mine came from a lady who lived in a house just outside the Zoo grounds, backing on to the lions' enclosure. On a warm summer evening, with the windows wide open, she answered a phone call. As she listened to the person at the other end of the phone Ross roared, making conversation difficult. 'Excuse me a moment,' she said, 'I'll close the window, the lions are particularly noisy this evening.'

After Ross's death, Lizzie, who was two years younger, was lonely. Lions are social animals, and it was obvious she was pining for her mate,

Blue and gold macaw parrot.

behaviour problems and, appealingly, a big personality. He went to a special needs school, and due to his sometimes difficult behaviour, required supervision. He was happiest when he was with animals, because they didn't recognize his disabilities, and he loved the Zoo, which was why we made him a junior keeper. During his school holidays and at weekends he helped with cleaning and feeding, and there were many times when he brought visitors into my office to meet his boss and show them his chair, which was located at the end of my desk.

Birds in Paradise

Zoos are for people, animals, reptiles... and birds. When Jon Blount introduced me to two blue and gold macaw parrots, I felt that something ominous was about to happen. The macaws had been kept in a small cage for so long that the muscles in their wings had atrophied and they couldn't fly. The only cage big enough to retrain them was my office, so to make them feel at home, the stationery room was adapted as their night-time residence, and during the day they had the freedom of the office. It was my job to retrain them to fly.

When they could, they were going to live in a large nest high in the cedar of Lebanon tree outside my office, which towered above the barren rocky area, where two radiated tortoises happily grazed in the peace and quiet of their desert island. When they became sufficiently confident, the macaws would have the freedom of the Zoo; then there would be parrots flying among the trees of our jungle, and tortoises roaming across the rocky desert.

Parrots in the wild chew trees. There were no trees in my office so they chewed the doors, window frames, partition walls and my ears. One of them decided that my shoulders provided an excellent perch from which to nibble an ear or two. As they grew stronger and braver, they flew from ledge to ledge and from my head to anyone else's who happened to be in the room. The bank manager, who was almost bald, didn't go much on it when he visited us. When one perched on his head to use as more than a take-off ledge, he was even less thrilled, although I cleaned him up and said it would bring him good luck.

It was two months before our birds got the hang of flying and we bid them goodbye. It was time to repair the damage. If two parrots could do so much damage to a small office, the South American rainforests stood no chance.

Their new home was ready for them in the cedar of Lebanon tree, a very precious and no doubt nervous tree that needed protection from our feathered friends. The macaws were locked in their nest, an old beer barrel, which we hoped they would look upon as home eventually, and return to each day for feeding and nesting.

A week later we unlocked the barrel door, but no parrot emerged. Eventually, one of them decided to step on to the balcony. It was the male, the largest of the two, and he seemed to be afraid of heights, which was not surprising, since both of them had been born in zoos and had no experience of being in high trees in a rainforest. He kept peering over the edge – a sign that he wanted to fly, but was afraid to do so. It must have been like standing on the high diving board of a swimming pool, wanting to jump off, but not daring to.

'Just a little jump and flap your wings.' He did. He spread his wings, took a leap out, and tombstoned into a pile of sand below. Shaken, but not deterred, he dusted himself off and flew upwards with confidence. Flying up was no problem. He tried again, but this time he forgot to flap his wings. The female, having watched the debacle from the balcony, decided home was the safest place to be, and went back into the barrel.

When we lowered the barrel, they liked it much better, being only a short distance down to the ground. One after the other, they launched themselves, but, failing to flap their wings in a co-ordinated manner, they collapsed into the sand and stared into the faces of two bewildered radiated tortoises which had taken refuge on a nearby rock.

They could fly, but only up. Living outside and flying through trees was not for them, so they were moved to the long, rather than high, free-flight aviary with other birds. They flew up into not very tall trees, and climbed down using beaks and claws. This new contentment resulted in an egg, so we gave up trying to subject them to the misery of flying. The

The male, Bird Bird, so-called because of the local pidgin dialect's habit of saying a word and repeating it, had been the adopted pet of friends, an Australian couple who lived on the same island. In fact, Bird Bird had adopted the Australians, by flying into their house and deciding that it was a desirable place in which to live. When the Australians completed their tour of duty, they had entrusted him to the care of Tremar and Joan.

Cockatoos, being highly intelligent, are quick to accept friends, and Bird Bird became devoted to them. The local government agency for whom Joan worked had recently rescued a female blue-eyed sulphur-crested cockatoo from a sub-standard zoo in Papua New Guinea. Knowing of the care that Tremar and Joan were giving to Bird Bird, the agency gave the female to Joan, recognizing the importance of a breeding opportunity. Lady Bird became a member of the Menendez family.

One of the reasons why the government agency rescued the female from the zoo was that her wings had been pinioned – that is, her prime feathers had been cut back to prevent her flying away – a practice not encouraged, although it is often a temporary measure, since the pinioned feathers generally grow back. Lady Bird had been so severely pinioned she would never fly again. She needed the tender loving care of Tremar and Joan and, hopefully, Bird Bird.

Government agencies maintain strict control on wild animals kept as pets, and make regular inspections, especially of animals and birds on the endangered species list. Tremar and Joan were ideal foster parents who already had a male cockatoo of the same species.

In The Gambia, West Africa, people living in villages and compounds often kept parrots in cages outside their homes. The government passed a law forbidding this, and insisted that all cage doors should be opened, and the birds released. If the law was not obeyed, there would be heavy fines. So people obeyed; cage doors were opened, and the birds released. Some weeks later, when government inspectors visited the compounds, they found the cages still contained the parrots. Before heavy fines could be imposed, it was discovered that the birds had been released, but had returned to what they knew as their homes. There was no need to close cage doors any more. Tender loving care carried the day. Birds and people lived happily together.

Bird Bird was the extrovert of the pair of cockatoos: a celebrity in the settlements, and a favourite with the children at local schools. Lady Bird preferred a quiet life, enjoying Bird Bird's company only as long as there was a barrier between them, since her inability to fly meant she could not easily escape his amorous advances.

Despite Tremar and Joan's best endeavours, the lack of a lover's union meant the absence of Baby Bird. They hoped that a new environment in Cornwall might prove conducive to romance, so they donated the birds to the Zoo, and through their further generosity we built the Menendez Cockatoo Enclosure in the Oriental Garden. However, a new environment, special diets, the company of other birds, and regular visits from Tremar and Joan failed to produce an offspring.

There were other changes, though, and Bird Bird, previously the extrovert, became the introverted one of the pair, while Lady Bird thrived on the attention of visitors, and even laid two eggs to demonstrate her contentment. But without help from Bird Bird, the hoped-for breeding of first-generation chicks remained no more than a hope. Ultimately, we took the decision to split the pair: Lady Bird went to a male at Paradise Park in Hayle, and a new female came to Newquay.

Joan became ill soon after retiring to Cornwall and, sadly, after a short illness, she died. She's probably still close to Lady Bird and, who knows, there might yet be a Baby Bird.

Tremar still came to the Zoo, and talked to his cockatoo. Some years later, he married Kitty. Although there had been no 'chatter of tiny beaks', we'd made three wonderful friends. Tremar and Kitty often visit Jenny and me, and Joan has a special place in our memory.

*

What should be done with cash in the bank? To be successful, a company needs to make profit, but what is important is what is done with the profit. Wanting to develop the Zoo further, we decided to spend it.

Our development plans included creating a new Children's Farm; renovating and extending the penguins' enclosure, and refurbishing the raccoons' enclosure. Profit and further borrowing enabled this to happen. Soon we had completed the Children's Farm, and the other work was well under way.

Arabian spiny mouse.

Themed on farmyards around the world, the new Children's Farm was home to owls, rats, mice, chickens, ducks, goats, pigs, sheep, a llama, and Zebedee, a zebu. A zebu is a small cow with a hump on its shoulders, and in India is looked upon as a sacred cow. Zebedee's mother had died giving birth, so I hand-reared him. He considered me to be his mother, and would nuzzle my arm whenever he saw me approach his enclosure. Not many people hand-rear a zebu.

Snowy owl.

arrested and taken to the local police station, which was probably more to protect the kangaroo from further injury than to lock up Mrs Eade.

With Di out of the way, probably in a cell, the bear, lion and gorilla, confidently handed out leaflets which allegedly showed the predicament in which many animals in zoos found themselves.

It's amazing what distortions can be made by cutting, pasting, and using computer-generated information. We provided bins for any visitors who had been given unwanted litter. The CAPS members didn't stay long, possibly fearing Mrs Eade's return and, despite my invitation to come into the Zoo, have coffee and put their points of view to any visitors wishing to listen, they drove off. It was a funny sight, the gorilla was driving.

Not long after they left, the police phoned and said they'd decided not to charge Di with assaulting a kangaroo, and she would be ready to come back as soon as she'd finished her cup of tea.

The headline in the newspaper a few days later said she'd 'kicked the kangaroo in the pouch'.

Dining Out with a Friend

When the weather became warmer we took the tortoises out of the fridge where they'd spent the winter, and put them in their new tortoise-shaped enclosure near the sign that said 'The penguin pool is being renovated'.

Keeping them in the fridge at a controlled temperature slowed their body functions and blood temperature, allowing them to live off stored fat during their period of hibernation, and emerge fit and well in time to entertain our visitors. Tortoises are great entertainers: watch them knocking seven bells out of each others' shells. I'm not sure whether it's due to friendship, anger, sexual excitement, or a combination of all three.

The 'being-renovated' penguin pool had now been renovated, and was going to be officially opened by Rolf Harris. All the members of the Junior Penguin Club, run by Mark Norris and Wendy Winstanley, were going to be stewards on the day, and Rolf would give autographed photographs to each of them. There were thirty members in the club, but by the time Rolf came there were sixty. The news of a visiting celebrity had spread to the far corners of Newquay, especially to would-be Junior Penguins.

On the day of his visit, sixty Junior Penguin Club members (how did they get to look so smart?) lined up at the entrance to greet him. We'd done a roaring trade in the sale of Penguin Club sweaters that morning. Rolf was ushered in via the exit, where formal introductions were made. Alwen, Rolf's wife, asked me to take care of him.

Out in the Zoo grounds there were a thousand Rolf Harris fans waiting to see him, or better still, to touch him. Alwen had seen it all before. On the way to the new pool, I showed him the 'able-to-withstand-a-nuclear-bomb-blast' primate cages, now suitably enriched with trampolines and

Rolf Harris opens the new Penguin Pool.

enjoyed by contented monkeys; the Zoo hospital, and the African plains where zebra, antelopes and porcupines grazed, and 'kneecaps' stood on sentry duty. Running the gauntlet of the waiting fans, we made our way past the old bear pit, now a luxury enclosure where Hemlock and his family were busy digging for hidden mealworms.

At the penguin pool were Peru and nine other penguins, which, in still unmelodic unison, greeted Rolf, who was carrying a bucket of sprats. It was the power of fish that did it. As he threw the fish into the water, the penguins dived and swam after them, while Rolf, using a lapel microphone, announced the opening of the pool.

Peru was not in awe of the celebrity in their midst; Rolf was just the man who fed her. She waited at the gate at the end of feeding time for the usual 'walkabout', but with more than a thousand people wanting to be close to Rolf Harris, Peru was not the star of the show this time. A squashed penguin would not be a pretty sight.

The return journey was slow, because Rolf often stopped to sign autograph books thrust at him. Eventually, we reached the Village Farm where, with our ten-foot-long Burmese python wound around him, and Iggy, our male iguana, draped casually across his shoulder, he sang several verses of 'Two Little Boys', and was joined in the chorus by a thousand voices.

By the time Rolf and Alwen, the Mayors of Restormel and Newquay and invited VIPs, had lunched and departed, it had been an exciting day. Sixty very tired Junior Penguin Club members went home clutching their autographed photos. Visitors – many of whom had travelled a great distance to see Rolf – had not been disappointed.

Our lion was still sick. Major, now very lame, had not responded to conventional medical treatment. People had heard of his problem, and offered help.

A healer, Len Cervi, and a local chiropractor both used their skills while Major was under anaesthetic and, believing that it might be arthritis, a company that supplied copper bracelets successful in alleviating pain in humans, made a special bracelet for him. He must have been the only lion ever to wear a bracelet around his ankle. A visitor to the Zoo on holiday with her family had noticed his instability, but more than that, she was a faith healer and said she had been made aware of Lizzie's sadness by her guiding spirit.

Although the lions enjoyed a close relationship and were constant companions, Major's condition had set them apart from each other. When cats are ill, they seek solitude, and now Major spent much of his time alone in a corner of the enclosure.

Our faith healer, Marie, wanted to transfer energy from Lizzie to him, so on each day of her holiday, she sat outside the enclosure using her powers of mental transference. If conventional medicine, difficult and dangerous to administer, did not work, we were willing to try any alternatives.

I believed that such remedies could work in the right circumstances, but despite everyone's best efforts, Major got worse. He had difficulty in standing; frequently lost his balance; was not eating, and, alarmingly, had become 'glassy eyed'. It was a condition Mike King, our vet, had seen in sick cows. Major's symptoms were similar to Bovine Spongiform Encephalitis (BSE), also known as Mad Cow Disease. In humans it is known as Creutzfeldt-Jakob Disease (CJD), named after the German doctors who discovered it.

In cats, it is Feline Spongiform Encephalitis (FSE), similar to Mad Cow Disease and part of a family of diseases called TSEs (Transmissable Spongiform Encephalopathies). It affects the central nervous system through diseased prions – proteins present in the nervous systems of all mammals. Their exact function is not known and, although it is extremely rare, prions, when they are diseased, form clusters in the brain. When brain cells die, the diseased prions create holes that convert the brain into a sponge-like substance. Hence Spongiform.

When Major's condition deteriorated and it became obvious that curing him was not possible, our options were exhausted. We had to do what was right for him. To see such a wonderful animal in a distressed state, which would soon get worse, was not acceptable. He was a gentle giant who needed to exit with dignity. FSE was confirmed a few days later by Vic Simpson at the County Veterinary Investigation Centre in Truro, when he had performed an autopsy.

In the interest of other carnivores in the Zoo, we needed to find out how Major had contracted the disease. He had come to us from Longleat, where, as in other wildlife parks, lions roamed free in many acres and lived in 'as-close-to-the-wild' conditions as possible. There it was deemed natural to feed whole carcasses of animals, which would provide a balanced nutritional diet without need for any supplements. In fact, they lived and fed much as they did in the wild in their natural habitats.

The carcasses fed to the animals were mostly fallen stock of cattle, sheep, horses and deer. It was thought that Major had been unlucky enough to eat the brains and spinal cord of a cow that had diseased prions. It had an incubation period of some four or five years, so it occurred a long while before he came to Newquay Zoo.

Since it is a rarity, it was not likely that the other lions had eaten animals infected in this way. They showed no signs of the disease. Cows are predominantly vegetarians, but were fed bulk manufactured food supplement that contained animal body parts including offal, brains and spinal cords. Such contaminated food, in pellet or flake form, is no longer used.

Humans who contracted CJD probably did so by eating cheap, unchecked, processed meat, such as burgers and sausages that contained brains and spinal cords.

Sheep and deer were not subjected to processed food in this way, so avoided the disease as far as we know. Sheep, however, contracted a similar disease... Scrapie! By the time the source of the disease was discovered, much damage and suffering had occurred.

However, it is believed that through awareness and more rigorous Health and Safety regulations, the disease has now been eradicated. Brains and spinal cords are removed from animals used in any kind of food product.

Lizzie had now lost two mates.

However, Bob Trollope at Longleat agreed to help find a suitable male, which, ideally, would be of similar age and a sufficiently docile companion for an elderly lady.

Blockbuster

Two of our penguins had been offered parts in a new film. Although destined for stardom, they were reluctant to leave the security of their home, which had water, sand, rocks, vegetation and caves. Why leave nirvana? Through the persuasion of food, they were eventually tempted into a carry-cage to be transported to a beach in Charlestown, near St Austell, where actors, cameramen and an impatient film director awaited them.

The beach was a simulation of the wild and desolate coast of South America, and desolation didn't come more desolate than on a windswept winter day in a howling gale in Charlestown. As the cameras rolled, a rowing boat containing eight shipwrecked sailors was tossed up on to the sand and rocks by the frothing waves.

warning not to come to Cornwall. Car-parks remained empty, as did the extra buses brought in to help the envisaged transport problem. There was no need for the services of more police and traffic wardens, so they were stood down.

Fields that had been prepared for caravans and tents became empty, soggy quagmires, turned into paddy fields by the heavy overnight rain and the churning wheels of lorry-loads of Cornwall's new logo.

The Zoo had it second quietest 11 August since we bought the lease. The few of us who were in Cornwall that day looked skywards at the appointed time of 11:00 am, hoping to see darkness.

Many of my staff missed it, although a couple of optimists laid claim to having seen it. Courtney Eustice, who had been with me at The Seal Sanctuary and had had to retire due to his age, had come to work at the Zoo three years previously in the maintenance department. He said he didn't know what all the fuss was about. He was in the tool shed when it happened, and had the light on anyway because there were no windows.

Marc Moase had been in the village farm, and said that the animals got ready to sleep thinking it was night time. Marc saw things that others didn't.

What should have been the event of a lifetime, turned out to be an expensive, damp and cloudy anticlimax. But that evening, I appeared on television to talk about the effect of the eclipse on the animals. The watching world needed to hear about the sensational things that did happen.

I told them that all the meerkats stood to attention and looked skywards, fearing an attack by predators, and that a flock of geese, gathered on the path to prepare for their usual early-evening flight around the Zoo, aborted their runway take-off because it suddenly got dark.

People were of the opinion that the Zoo was a wonderful place to study animal behaviour during an eclipse, so I didn't want to disappoint them. I said that Marc Moase thought the animals in the village farm were going to sleep, but I didn't mention that Courtney missed it all because he was in the tool shed and had the light on since there were no windows.

A few weeks later, there was hardly a trace of the eclipse, not that there had been much anyway. Lorries took away the Portaloos; the warehouses of food got eaten, and the fields were given back to the sheep, cows and crops. The only signs left were the granite boulders in gateways and entrances. A year later they were still there. No one could get in or out of the fields. Things happen 'dreckly' (a little less urgently than *mañana*) in Cornwall.

*

Fortunately, no one had put any boulders at the entrance to the field where one day a new college would be home to zoological students.

Mike Kent, the press and I watched as the Mayor, armed with a ceremonial shovel, turned the first sod. Many more sods would have to be turned before the students sat at their desks.

Rosalie and Norman Cooper's golden wedding anniversary party at the Zoo.

I watched the piece of turf on the Mayor's shovel being photographed from all angles, and realized just how far we had progressed since the early days of beckoning bankruptcy. The Zoo now employed forty staff; brought visitors and income into the county; played a substantial role in education; provided entertainment, and was accepted as a place of excellence for animals and people.

That was why we were chosen to be one of the six finalists in The National Small Business of The Year Award competition sponsored by The Department of Trade and Industry (DTI), HSBC (bank) and the BBC (British Broadcasting Corporation).

*

But before the award ceremony, I had to attend to several other matters. The first was organizing the golden wedding anniversary party of our first season-ticket holder… Norman Cooper. A marquee was erected on the lawn next to the African hut, overlooking the lake. The guests wore badges saying 'We're with the Coopers', and Norman and Rosalie's badges stated 'We are the Coopers'.

When the party finished, Jenny and I went to Crete for a short holiday. After an overnight flight and an early breakfast, we went down to the beach for what was to be a rest in the sun. I only moved the sun-bed out of the shade, when… snap went my ankle… for the third time. Without emergency treatment at the hospital in Aghios Nickolaos, great care and attention from our good friend Maria Sarafi, a manager at Elounda Beach Hotel, and sustenance from Dmitris at The Kafenion, the next three days of the holiday would not have been as memorable and comfortable as they were. I can think of no better place to break an ankle.

Four days later, after a first class flight courtesy of Olympic Airways, where even my broken ankle had a seat of its own, and an ambulance service all the way to Cornwall, Jenny and I were back at the Zoo and I was running the business from a wheelchair. My NatWest travel insurance did me proud.

It proved to be a very short holiday.

Telling the doctor at the hospital that I broke my ankle by pulling a sun-bed into the sun in Crete was not something to shout about. 'Not many people do that,' he said.

I had broken my ankle three times, not one of which was in a conventional way.

I did manage to have the plaster removed in time for the award ceremony however, but not before I was called upon to help my staff retrieve some escaped animals.

A wheelchair can be useful when speed is called for, and this was one such occasion. Mike, our Asian short-clawed otter, with his mate Jenny (I was told that any reference to the boss and his wife was co-incidental), sought refuge near the café after a cloudburst had caused their pond in the Oriental Garden to flood. Not wishing to experience the wrath of gushing water, they made a break for it, as far as the ice-cream kiosk, where they hid, hopefully safe from the storm.

I stood guard, or rather sat guard in my wheelchair, outside the ice-cream kiosk, ready to give chase, while keepers tried to coax them out with strips of fish. Jenny was first to succumb to the lure of food, and was soon caught; but Mike stayed where he was, of the opinion that danger lurked on all sides.

When it became dark, we shut Jenny back in her nest in the Oriental Garden, hoping she wouldn't take the chance of leaving home again alone. We put Mike's favourite food – chicken – in a trap under the kiosk, believing that hunger would lead him to it, and when it did the gate of the trap would spring shut behind him.

The staff went home, confident that he would be returned to Jenny the following day. But the next morning there was no sign of him or the chicken, and the trap was still set; no gate had sprung shut.

A check on the nest in the Oriental Garden found them both asleep, the remains of the chicken scattered around them. We should have called him Houdini.

*

Jenny and I met Mike Pulley, our bank manager, at the Blue Water Conference Centre, where the National Small Business of the Year award ceremony was to take place. Out of 150 businesses nationwide, the Zoo was one of six finalists chosen to be at the prestigious award ceremony, attended by business delegates, MPs, press and television companies.

Just to be recognized as a successful business would have been enough, but when Newquay Zoo's name was called as a winner, tears of emotion and pride were not far away. The award (second place) was a first for a South West of England company, and a first for a zoo. It was a deserved accolade for the staff in Newquay.

After tea, interviews and photo calls we caught the train home, weighed down by an inscribed

With Mike Pulley, bank manager (right), at the Small Business Award ceremony.

silver plate, a certificate, a cheque for two thousand pounds, and happiness. When we got back to the Zoo, we displayed the certificate and silver plate on the wall inside the Tropical House, alongside the increasing number of award certificates. This was where I was interviewed by Chris Blount of Radio Cornwall. It was also where I heard the Beta alarm call on my internal radio. Randy had left the Zoo.

Mrs Griffiths' Roast Potatoes

Randy, a raccoon, had been an exper-ienced escapologist before he was arrested by the RSPCA and brought to the Zoo. He had made nightly raids on fish ponds on an estate in Exeter, which had displeased the fish-loving residents there.

At the Zoo he joined five raccoons in a new enclosure, complete with waterfall, stream, pond and trees, where the others were contentedly enjoying an environment that was safe and provided regular meals. Randy had other ideas, and looked for a way out to adventures new.

Raccoons are great foragers, and our visitors delighted in watching them at feeding times, rummaging in strategically placed dustbins in their enclosure, and cleaning their food in the stream. They are shy, timid ani-

Now, how do I get the lid off this bin?

mals and pose no great danger to humans. Their favourite food is fish and chicks, and there was a plentiful supply of these in the neighbourhood, so I reckoned that any fish and chicks living nearby would be fair game to Randy.

Hoping his escape would not precipitate a mass breakout, the enclosure was checked for any faults in the hot wires.

Courtney, Zoo 16, whom I asked to check the enclosure on my radio, answered me, 'Yes, my love?'

'Courtney, I am your boss, not your love.'

There were no faults in the wires, so no danger of a mass breakout. The hunt for Randy was on.

Raccoons have dark rings around their eyes, which make them look like masked burglars. They are nocturnal, so are rarely seen. In their native North America they enjoy nothing better than raiding urban bins in search of easy food.

Jane and Mike Griffiths and their daughters lived not far from the Zoo, and their bin had been raided, which was a likely sign of Randy's presence. For the next three weeks, night raids on the Griffiths' bin became regular occurrences, and once Randy was seen in torchlight by Mike Griffiths, who agreed to keep a nightly lookout.

We set traps with tempting bits of fish and slices of chicken, but by the end of the first week the trap had caught three cats and a badger. Randy preferred the Griffiths' bin. Keepers and volunteers scoured the neighbourhood, looking up into tree tops, which were raccoons' favourite sleeping places by day.

But elusive Randy was only ever seen by the Griffith family, who now enjoyed his nightly forays so much that gazing at their bin at night had superseded television as their evening entertainment.

What had been thought to be Randy's favourite foods, fish and chicks, were enjoyed by six neighbourhood cats, two grey squirrels and an inquisitive puppy. The cats were pleased to be released from the traps; the squirrels took a bit of persuasion to leave and, locating the owner of the puppy – an elderly lady in the next street – pleased us, her, and the ecstatic dog.

By now Randy was sleeping off the contents of the Griffiths' bin somewhere in the branches of a high tree. Two keepers spent a night in a tent, using infrared lamps waiting for him, but he didn't show up. He'd been ambushed before, and wasn't going to fall for it again.

The next night he was seen by Jane and Mike Griffiths. He was obviously particular about whose company he was seen in. It was getting near to holiday time, and the Griffiths family wanted Randy to stay escaped so that he could have Christmas dinner out of their bin.

Although he missed the Revd Peter Long's sixth Christmas with the Animals Carol Service, attended by two hundred visitors, he did come home in time for the New Year's celebrations. It was Christmas dinner that did the trick. Jane had put the leftovers in the bin, and added a few extra roast potatoes. 'After all it is Christmas!' Randy 'the night bandit' ventured forth in the dead of night. The next day the bin was on its side in their garden, and emptied of Christmas dinner. That night we put some roast potatoes in a trap. Next morning, Randy was found fast asleep, door shut tight, with not a roast potato in sight.

After a period of solitary confinement back at the Zoo, he was allowed to rejoin the gang. When the Griffiths family came the following weekend, Jane brought him a present. He ate the lot.

Grinners in the Mist

Randy's return heralded an auspicious occasion... the dawning of a new millennium... 1 January 2000. To celebrate it and greet our visitors, my smiling staff stood at the entrance to the Zoo holding a banner saying 'WELCOME TO NEWQUAY ZOOO'.

Tables on the patio were laden with specially made millennium cake, and glasses of champagne were full, ready to toast the birth of the decade. We expected many people to come on this cold, crisp, important day.

However, first to arrive was the famous Cornish winter mist, which, egged on by an increasing wind, swirled around, enveloping the staff, the welcome banner, cakes, champagne, and most of the Zoo.

'I couldn't see a hand in front of my face,' Geoff said. It was unlikely that many would be celebrating the momentous occasion with us in weather like this. Champagne and cake were enjoyed mostly by the staff.

But the new millennium was not prepared to roll over and lie down. Nor were we. The many sunny days from the end of January provided a reminder that spring was within touching distance.

So was Ronnie. Cheski and I stood at the keeper's entrance and watched Bob Trollope and Keith, in a Longleat Land Rover, drive towards us.

The new king had arrived, but first he had to spend a few days in solitary confinement. His home was to be his crate in the enclosure. Lizzie had been 'tucked away' in the den without dissent, complaint or hesitation. It was as if she knew that another romance was on the cards.

The invasion of the media, which for us was always good pub-

In the millennium mist.

Marc's Arc

Caring for animals and for people took twenty-four hours a day, three hundred and sixty-five days a year. That was why we owned a zoo.

When I had a phone call one evening from the children's ward at Treliske hospital, I had no difficulty recognizing the voice of Marc Moase. Marc didn't need a telephone. He'd had an asthmatic attack, but was feeling better and he wanted to let me know that he would be coming to the Zoo as soon as he was out of hospital.

A few days later he had another asthmatic attack. He was thirteen when he died.

His chair stood at the end of my desk as a reminder of a dear friend who had been in our world for just thirteen years. His parents wanted to keep his uniform and badge, since they belonged to him and would always be part of his memory.

Instead of flowers at the funeral, Marc's parents asked that donations should be made to the Zoo. This was the beginning of Marc's Arc, a charitable trust which we established to help children with learning difficulties.

Through the trust, over the years, Jenny and I have been able to help those in need. Due to the generosity of many people, in particular Dave and Anne Moase; my parents-in-law, Cecil and Doreen Weston; Les and Betty Blackett; my co-director, Roger Martin; Brownie; Mrs Watkins; Steven, who rode a unicycle around the county to raise funds; our staff, and several legacies, the charity, now renamed The Arc Trust, has broadened its mission statement to include assistance for sick and disabled children in Cornwall.

Marc left us the best legacy: the ability to help others. He was not far away.

A French poet, Victor Hugo, who lost his daughter, Léopoldine, when she drowned in a boating accident while on honeymoon, wrote,

'*Il faut que l'herbe pousse et que les enfants meurent*'

'For grass must grow and children die.'

*

Life doesn't end; it's only one stage of it that's over, but it is those who are left behind who feel the sadness most. I felt it when Courtney died. He and I had been together for many years, first at The Seal Sanctuary, then at the Zoo.

He was on late maintenance duty, and when the Zoo closed for the day he was pressure-hosing the pathways – a job he enjoyed, because he could stop to talk to the animals. We all talked to the animals, but Courtney always had a lot to say to them, which was why pressure-hosing took him so long.

Di Eade was in the office and called Zoo 16 on the radio several times. There was no response.

Mike Bungard, the senior keeper on lock-up duty, found him sitting on the grass, leaning against the puma enclosure fence. He thought he was asleep. He died in the place he loved, among friends... animals and humans.

When I went to his funeral to say goodbye, it was not as 'his love' or his boss, but as a friend who had valued his presence. It was good to know that he'd spent his last few minutes on earth with the pumas, his favourite animals, which, at last were in their new enclosure at the far end of the Zoo.

*

The 'on the back of a fag packet' initial design sketches for their enclosure, done by Jon Blount and my son Ben, had eventually been translated into high-quality drawings and plans by an architect friend, Jonathan Ball, who practised in North Cornwall, and the enclosure was built by Gordon Derry & Son of Wadebridge.

The enclosure had three storeys: a basement consisting of sleeping and isolation quarters; a ground floor leading to an open area of grass, trees, shrubs, pond and stream, and an upper deck approached via a rock face and tree trunks.

Pumas are also called mountain lions, due to their ability to climb and jump. They inhabit the rocky, desolate areas of North America, although some sub-species are found as far south as Florida.

Jenny Agutter opens the new puma enclosure.

The unique feature of this enclosure was that it was open to the sky, there was no roof. Due to pumas' agility, and ability to climb and jump great heights, a traditional enclosure always had a roof, but, by angling the pillars at the top by 45° and hot-wiring them, we dispensed with the need for this.

One of the highlights of a visit to the Zoo was feeding-time for the pumas, when they demonstrated their agility by leaping for meat suspended from short ropes attached to longer ropes on a pulley system high above them. The pulleys enabled the food to be pulled along at different speeds in different directions, which replicated moving prey and encouraged natural behaviour.

This enclosure won another award for the Zoo, and was officially opened, in wet and windy weather, by the actress Jenny Agutter, in the presence of the press, many visitors and a group of disabled children, who were very wet, but very happy.

Courtney's name is on a plaque at the pumas' enclosure.

I was pleased we owned a zoo.

HQ was all it was Cracked up to Be

Mike Pulley, our bank manager, had suggested that we should submit an application for The National Small Business of The Year Award 2000, in which we had won second place the previous year.

Winning it once was a wonderful achievement and a great honour, and when we heard that once more we had been chosen as one of the six finalists out of more than two hundred applicants nationwide, it was incredible. Our zoo had come a long way.

The award ceremony was held at HSBC's Head Offices in Canary Wharf, London. Jenny, Mike Pulley and I travelled by train from Truro, and were accommodated in five-star luxury in a hotel in St Katharine Docks.

During the afternoon, before the award presentation at dinner that evening, we were given a tour of HSBC's opulent offices by the chairman. I counted six Lowry originals, as well as other paintings and sculptures in the many oak-panelled boardrooms. Banks rule OK.

At a dinner presentation that evening, Newquay Zoo came fourth out of the six finalists.

On the way home to Cornwall the next day, we had lunch on the train. Although we hadn't won the award, a very excited bank manager was thrilled to have been to HQ.

Paw Prince

Once Upon a Time Big Cats Were Kittens

Zoo staff knew that if an animal escaped, they should at all times remain calm, not panic, and deal with the matter as if it were a routine procedure... expect the unexpected. Panicking would spook an already anxious and stressed animal.

Not wanting to be spooked myself, I didn't panic when I heard the news bulletin that told the whole of Cornwall that a taxi driver had the fright of his life when, on his way to work early in the morning, in his headlights he saw two kangaroos bounding down a street in Newquay.

I realized straight away that the kangaroos were wallabies that had 'done a runner' from where they lived and roamed free in the grounds of Newquay Zoo. Although their way out had to be discovered, their safe return was the most pressing priority. Gamma alert warnings – since the animals were not dangerous – were relayed to staff on duty, some of whom already knew of the incident, having heard it from the coastguard giving the shipping forecast on the radio much earlier that morning. He made a point of saying that they posed no danger to ships in the area.

One of the wallabies on its return to the Zoo.

Two of our keepers, armed only with a net, scoured the deserted streets, realizing that the wallabies should be caught before the busy morning traffic got under way, to avoid the possibility of accidents.

Jenny and I reached the Zoo in record time. All was calm and staff were on their usual morning rounds. When the keepers' entrance gates at the side of the Zoo were opened, two wallabies were waiting to be let in. It was breakfast time. They had got out through a gate left open by a 'soon-to-be-dismissed' subcontractor, who had been working in the grounds.

The taxi driver who had had the kangaroo fright brought his family to see what he now knew were wallabies. I told him that if they had a baby, we'd name it after him. Arthur was born in June that year. She was beautiful.

Many years ago, wallabies had escaped from a private collection in Hampshire, bred and started a new population in the countryside. Coypu did the same in Norfolk. It was good to get our wallabies back, since the last thing we wanted was a lot of little Arthurs jumping around Newquay.

*

The 'Beast of Bodmin' – a typical photo.

Animals escape, and some stay escaped, such as the Beast of Bodmin, alias the Beast of Exmoor, the Beast of Birmingham, the Beast of Wales, and the Beast of Everywhere Else. He (why is it always 'he'?), roamed East Anglia, Scotland and Ireland too. It seemed 'he' was a long-distance traveller of great age.

'I've seen him,' was a regular call to the Zoo. Sometimes 'he' was black, sometimes brown and once white. The white one was a goat.

I was called to the scene of a sighting of a lion in Devon, which even initiated a police helicopter search. The police had to respond to such a sighting, but my money was on a Great Dane that lived not far from the scene of the crime. Nothing was found, so I supposed that the Great Dane was keeping his head down.

Lying on my desk was a video that had been brought in by the police. It was a film of a big cat. Pumas are suspects, and Newquay Zoo had three pumas. Could I compare the one in the film with ours?

I was 'the Big Cats in the wild' expert, called out to examine evidence of sightings. Over a period of ten years, I recorded more than two hundred.

Sightings have been reported as far back as the 1930s, but most have occurred since 1976, when The Dangerous Wild Animals Act came into force, which made it illegal, except in Ireland, for people to keep dangerous wild animals without a licence.

The conditions of the licence were strict and expensive, so many exotic 'pets' were suddenly unwanted and released, or escaped, as some would have it, into the 'wilds' of Britain, to fend for themselves.

Deserted moorlands, with plentiful supplies of food such as rabbits, birds, mice, sheep and deer, provided ideal homes for lynx and pumas in particular. Harsh winter climates were no deterrent to them. The European lynx, before its presumed extinction, was an indigenous species, as were wolves and bears.

With so many sightings of big cats from all over Britain, 'he' had to be 'them'. The lifespan of most big cats is about fifteen years, so they must have bred, and for that to happen there had to be 'hims' and 'hers'. Most of them that were reported were black.

Panthers are black, pumas are brown. However, panther is a generic term, which includes pumas. Despite there being no photographic evidence of the existence of black pumas, it is not to deny the fact that they may exist, since their colour varies throughout habitats in America.

Like most cats, pumas are predominantly nocturnal, hunting between dusk and dawn, so in the shadows, brown may appear black. Anyway, blackness is far more exciting and sinister. It is the sign of the devil.

I had not been prepared to agree that the sightings were of panthers until I saw Ebony at Exmoor Zoo in North Devon. The owners, Danny

Jethro, Newquay Zoo's brown puma (top). Ebony, Exmoor Zoo's black panther (above).

and Lyn Reynolds, invited me to give a talk to their visitors entitled 'The Beast of Exmoor'. Before I was due to talk I walked around the zoo, a great favourite of mine, and stopped at the Panther Enclosure. Ebony was not far away. She stood in typical cat position, hunched and poised for the kill. Her green, menacing, hypnotic eyes held me spellbound and sent a shiver down my spine. I realized what it must be like to be her intended prey.

This beautiful, awesome creature fitted exactly the many descriptions I had been given over the years. But so did pumas fit the descriptions.

Having spoken to someone, who knew someone who had released pumas into the wild, I was prepared to accept reports of sightings without question. Except in colour, pumas and panthers are similar.

WANTED... Big Cat.

Big cat casts (left). Paw prints (right).

one in the photograph. It was a fox, had pointed ears, a bushy tail and had, possibly unbeknown to the gentleman, been 'doctored'. It was a hoax photograph, one of many that came my way over the years.

I often received photographs of paw prints which were far too large to be those of big cats or big dogs, but in soft ground paw prints spread, exaggerating the size. One photograph I received, with a note attached to it said... 'This paw print measures seven inches by five inches.' Had this been genuine, we would have been looking for a monster!

During my time as the Big Cat Expert, I collected photographs of paw prints, clay casts and plaster casts, but the most unusual one came following a phone call informing me that a big cat had been seen in a field, and the caller had found a paw print. He had posted the evidence to me, and would welcome my opinion.

Putting One's Foot in It

A few days later, a box arrived, and inside was the paw print of the big cat which had been left in what I was holding... a dried-out cowpat.

Often, through the post, came photographs or plaster casts of paw prints, without any consideration that the animal which owned them had four legs. If distances between front and back legs had been measured, it might have been possible to obtain an idea of the size of the animal. However, if the sender of the cowpat print had followed this advice, he would have needed a very productive cow with a good aim, and an obliging big cat which didn't mind where it trod.

Deserted moorlands, with plentiful supplies of food such as rabbits, birds, mice, sheep and deer, provided ideal homes for lynx and pumas in particular. Harsh winter climates were no deterrent to them. The European lynx, before its presumed extinction, was an indigenous species, as were wolves and bears.

With so many sightings of big cats from all over Britain, 'he' had to be 'them'. The lifespan of most big cats is about fifteen years, so they must have bred, and for that to happen there had to be 'hims' and 'hers'. Most of them that were reported were black.

Panthers are black, pumas are brown. However, panther is a generic term, which includes pumas. Despite there being no photographic evidence of the existence of black pumas, it is not to deny the fact that they may exist, since their colour varies throughout habitats in America.

Like most cats, pumas are predominantly nocturnal, hunting between dusk and dawn, so in the shadows, brown may appear black. Anyway, blackness is far more exciting and sinister. It is the sign of the devil.

I had not been prepared to agree that the sightings were of panthers until I saw Ebony at Exmoor Zoo in North Devon. The owners, Danny

Jethro, Newquay Zoo's brown puma (top). Ebony, Exmoor Zoo's black panther (above).

and Lyn Reynolds, invited me to give a talk to their visitors entitled 'The Beast of Exmoor'. Before I was due to talk I walked around the zoo, a great favourite of mine, and stopped at the Panther Enclosure. Ebony was not far away. She stood in typical cat position, hunched and poised for the kill. Her green, menacing, hypnotic eyes held me spellbound and sent a shiver down my spine. I realized what it must be like to be her intended prey.

This beautiful, awesome creature fitted exactly the many descriptions I had been given over the years. But so did pumas fit the descriptions.

Having spoken to someone, who knew someone who had released pumas into the wild, I was prepared to accept reports of sightings without question. Except in colour, pumas and panthers are similar.

WANTED… Big Cat.

Round, squat face.

Rounded ears, not pointed as in domestic cats.

Tail – carried in a curve away from its body, ending in a 'bob'.

Territorial range about twenty miles.

Most likely seen dusk to dawn.

Solitary animal.

Size – varies according to age and sex.

Colour – brown, or darker shades thereof, even black.

These cats are secretive, shy animals, they are not 'loveable, strokable pussies', but unless trapped, injured or frightened, would be unlikely to attack a person.

Humans are likely to be more dangerous than big cats, which will avoid danger, knowing that if they were injured, they would not be able to hunt and would most likely starve. Being strong, agile and fast they are capable of killing large animals the size of an adult stag deer, but not wishing to face aggression, they would be more likely to opt for small prey such as lambs, rabbits, rodents and birds, which are plentiful in the countryside. Humans are considered to be in the large category, and best avoided. Nor are humans their favourite food, so, given a choice, they would look for something more to their taste.

Although I recorded reports of every sighting, many were not able to be followed up, for several reasons. For example, how long ago was the cat seen; at what distance was it seen, and what size was it?

'I saw a puma last week, in the daytime. It was about a hundred yards away, jumped over the hedge, and ran into the woods. It was black.'

'How big was it?'

'It was six feet long and three feet high.'

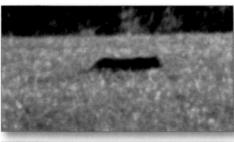

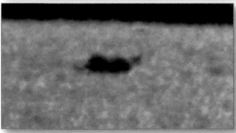

Photos taken at 100 metres distance.

It was like the story of the fish that got away, and got bigger every time the story was told. If it was black, it was likely to be a panther, and panthers are smaller than pumas. A large, adult male puma could grow to a length of four feet, and would probably be no more than two feet in height. From a distance of a hundred yards, it would be impossible to scale its size and with nothing to measure it against, it would look big. A crow in a field fifty yards away looks enormous. Perspective is deceptive.

Furthermore, a sighting made a week ago would leave no traces of hair; it would have been blown away in the wind. Any visible paw prints would have been washed away by the rain. To be worth further investigation, it needed to be reported within an hour and investigated soon afterwards.

'Why don't we ever see dead ones?' was a frequently asked question. Cats, instinctively, when sick or injured, find isolated areas where they often die. When dead, they become carrion for other animals; bones are picked clean, and eventually the remaining bits are bleached by weather. There are many bleached bones in isolated spots. I have found quite a few but, like most people, have never given much thought to the animals that owned them.

As far as most people are concerned, big cats have to be big, the bigger the better. Little cats don't count. Big cats are lions, tigers, pumas, panthers, leopards and cheetahs, and when seen in the wild in Britain, in order to be newsworthy, they must be at least six feet long.

A few years ago, a film given to me, taken over a period of a couple of weeks, was shown on a local television news programme. The person who took the film was genuinely convinced that what he saw were not domestic cats. They were black, which may have discounted their being pumas, but they displayed unusual behaviour. They were muscular, and had round ears, and tails that ended in 'bobs'. Admittedly, both of them were small. This cast doubt in the mind of the newscaster, who proceeded to give me a bit of a grilling.

He went on to say that his aunty's cat, Jemima, was bigger than those in the film. He had a point. 'Little cats in the wild' didn't have the same ring to it.

Nevertheless, big cats start out in life as kittens, and kittens are little. In time they would grow. Had this film been taken a year later, he might have changed his mind, and Jemima would have paled into insignificance. But evidence presented so far, although much of it has been significant, has been inconclusive, open to interpretation, and certainly good fodder for the doubters.

While the 'Big Cat Expert' had to be prepared to accept the scorn, doubt and negative views of the sceptics, sightings needed to be investigated, and the findings made public. The skull of a big cat found by two boys in a stream in Devon was declared by a curator at London Zoo to be that of a puma. It was indeed a puma, but scientific analysis proved it had been part of a rug that had once adorned a floor.

On one occasion, I received a photograph of a big cat which looked suspiciously like a fox. It was far too big to be a fox, but not clear enough to make a definitive judgement. I borrowed a 'stuffed' fox from the Royal Cornwall Museum in Truro, and together with the gentleman who had taken the photograph and a daily newspaper photographer, went to the location where he'd taken it. We put our long-dead animal on the hedge, in the position where he had seen it, returned to the position from where the photograph had been taken, and took another, using the same camera. The result was not what he had expected.

Our fox was no more than a dot on the horizon. But, by enlarging it, using special equipment, the animal appeared to be the same size as the

Big cat casts (left). Paw prints (right).

one in the photograph. It was a fox, had pointed ears, a bushy tail and had, possibly unbeknown to the gentleman, been 'doctored'. It was a hoax photograph, one of many that came my way over the years.

I often received photographs of paw prints which were far too large to be those of big cats or big dogs, but in soft ground paw prints spread, exaggerating the size. One photograph I received, with a note attached to it said… 'This paw print measures seven inches by five inches.' Had this been genuine, we would have been looking for a monster!

During my time as the Big Cat Expert, I collected photographs of paw prints, clay casts and plaster casts, but the most unusual one came following a phone call informing me that a big cat had been seen in a field, and the caller had found a paw print. He had posted the evidence to me, and would welcome my opinion.

Putting One's Foot in It

A few days later, a box arrived, and inside was the paw print of the big cat which had been left in what I was holding… a dried-out cowpat.

Often, through the post, came photographs or plaster casts of paw prints, without any consideration that the animal which owned them had four legs. If distances between front and back legs had been measured, it might have been possible to obtain an idea of the size of the animal. However, if the sender of the cowpat print had followed this advice, he would have needed a very productive cow with a good aim, and an obliging big cat which didn't mind where it trod.

Councillor Joan Vincent, with paw prints in soft clay.

But even single plaster casts told me a great deal. It was possible to estimate the weight of the animal by the depth of the print; whether it had been made by a cat or a dog, and whether it was a left or right paw print. A big cat moves with its claws retracted into the pads of its feet because it needs its claws for hunting. They are precious 'tools', which need to be looked after. I have found claw marks on trees where a cat had used the trunk to keep its claws sharpened.

A dog, being domesticated and not needing to hunt for food, does not have the same need for its claws, so does not retract or sharpen them. They are rarely used, and are mostly round-ended and blunt.

When Joan Vincent, chairman of Restormel Council, phoned to say that she and other councillors, travelling by coach along a road bordering the clay pits of St Austell, had seen a big cat, I was prepared to investigate. A sighting by a coach full of councillors was not to be dismissed lightly.

It was also a fact that big cats had been seen many times in this area by workers in the clay pits. Some years earlier, I had seen a film which had been taken of a big cat running along the valley through the pits. This was big-cat country alright.

Although the cat was only seen for a short time, Joan was sure that she could show me paw prints it would have left in the light-coloured, soft clay.

We went to the spot where it had been seen. Everywhere were paw prints of all shapes and sizes, and they generally had blunt claws. This was St Austell's favourite dog-walking area.

However, the sighting was of interest to the media, since it had been made by councillors. Later that day, Joan and I travelled the 'big cat's'

Paw print in St Austell (left). Puma paw against human hand (right).

route with a posse of photographers and television cameramen, who followed while I searched for paw prints of a cat in the clay among those left by the many dogs on their daily walks.

I explained to the group what to look for, and everyone spread out in search of big prints without claws. I only mentioned big because bigness was exciting and created enthusiasm for the job being undertaken. I hoped there'd be more than one print, or some joker in the press gang might report that a one-legged cat had been that way. Joan said it was six feet long and about three feet high – music to the ears of the press.

Eventually, I was the bringer of good news: there were some prints worthy of investigation. They were big. Joan was sure they belonged to the animal we were looking for, and now the doubters among the press waited to hear pearls of wisdom from my lips. An eagle-eyed photographer pointed to claw marks. I explained that these claw marks were sharp, and had long points, not at all like a dog's claws. It was a cat that had extended its claws to balance on uneven ground when it jumped from the bank above.

I saw the raised eyebrows of disbelief, but it was the truth, a cat will do just that in order to steady itself. Had we struck gold in the clay pits?

The press photographers took a photograph of my hand next to the print, in order to compare its size. It was a big paw print against a small hand.

The next day, the local and national newspapers carried a photograph of my hand pressed into the clay next to a paw print of a giant cat with sharp claws. Mine was the most photographed hand ever seen in newspapers in Britain.

During the following few weeks, Joan Vincent and I journeyed forth among the clay pits in search of 'The Beast'. We had a most enjoyable time, saw lots of dogs and found lots of dogs' prints. But big cats are shy and they eluded us, until yet another 'positive' sighting, possibly of the same animal, seen fifteen miles away, took Jenny and me to a wooded valley on Bodmin Moor, not far from the clay pits.

Looking for a big cat.

With binoculars and a camera we drove to the woods with photographers from the *Daily Mail* and the *Daily Telegraph*. When we arrived we were not alone. At least eighty other binocular- and camera-clad individuals had beaten us to it. Had the news of 'The Beast' spread that quickly?

But it was not 'our' Beast that drew the crowd. They were birdwatchers, looking for the buff-breasted sandpiper, a rare American visitor to our shores, and the eighty were probably just an advance party. Soon the woods would be alive with the sounds of twitchers, and no self-respecting big cat would hang around with that crowd, even though a buff-breasted sandpiper would make a tasty dish before dinner.

Excitement... someone had seen the bird. Binoculars and cameras were pointed groundwards about fifty yards away. Training my binoculars in the same general direction, I couldn't see anything. I am no good with birds. A beak, a couple of wings, and covered with feathers – seen one and you've seen them all! Most of them are brown, which is not my favourite colour. I was best with something big, like a big cat. Not that I was having much luck with that either.

Ornithologists stood the best chance of spotting our big cat, being often out in remote places in all weathers, armed with enough equipment to see and photograph a big cat a mile away. So I had a word with them. But none had ever seen one, and I got the impression that they belonged to the Big Cat Doubting Society, and thought I was a bit of a 'nutter'.

We left the woods and the twitchers in the company of the rare American visitor. I never did find out what a buff-breasted sandpiper looked like, but the birdwatchers' intrusion into our woods had ruined any chance of a sighting that day.

Film of a big cat in the wild would be worth a fortune, and I might have just missed a chance of becoming rich. Any evidence to secure my financial security would have to be backed up by film, a photograph or, better still, a big cat. To find a cat, trap it and take it into captivity was not the plan, however. It would not be fair to an animal living happily in the wild to take it to the Zoo. Judging by all the sightings, a breeding programme for the species' survival wasn't necessary, so there would be no justification whatsoever. However, there could be a case for catching it in a trap, tranquillizing it, taking samples of hair and blood, measuring and photographing it, then setting it free. We had actually set such a trap in a mountainous area in Wales some years ago, following a reputable sighting, before we were informed that government regulations did not allow it. If caught, it would have to stay captive. Release was not possible, so film or photographs would have to do.

Reports kept coming in, and when a cat was seen on a nearby farm, the press and television cameramen picked me up at the Zoo in a mini-bus, to see if I could identify any signs. Twelve of us travelled to the scene, hoping it might be the big one… a major scoop for us all.

The farmer had been looking out of a window and saw, no more than thirty yards away, a big cat. He said 'it was black and huge'. The press loved it. Apparently his sheep had been restless all night, which made him think something was amiss. But I didn't find a hair, a paw print or any other big-cat sign in the area.

Being worthy of further investigation, it was decided that I would hide out in a nearby shed in case it came back. The press and television crew concealed themselves and their cameras at the bottom of the garden, and waited for a signal from me. I also had a CCTV camera with me, which I located on a post at the side of the shed. If the cat didn't come while we were there, it might return that night for its dinner.

The shed had seen better days; most of the tin roof had collapsed, but I managed to crawl inside and, through a gap which had been a window in its former days of glory, I could push my head out and get a good view of the surrounding fields and, hopefully, a photogenic cat. Brown or black I didn't care, but preferably big.

Big cat newspaper article.

A cat has an excellent sense of smell, so it was doubtful that it would venture anywhere near enough to where I and eleven press-men were smelling. Predictably, the cat was nowhere to be seen by the time we left.

However, dinner time could be during the night, and the CCTV camera was in place. The next day, in the local newspaper, there was an excellent photograph of me, my head sticking out of a hole in the shed, gazing anxiously across the fields. It looked as if I was waiting to be rescued from a shed whose roof had collapsed.

My need to find a big cat was becoming an obsession. Then, one day, out of the blue it seemed that my prayers were about to be answered. A man from The Midlands phoned from his mobile to say that he could see, in the distance, a big cat. He didn't say what colour, but it was answering the call of nature. When he reached the site of nature's call it was still warm. He must have touched it to find that out.

I asked him to scoop up a decent sized sample, put it in a jar, put the jar in an ice-filled Thermos flask, and send it to me by express courier service. Some hours later, the sample was with me, still fresh but chilled. It looked like a jar of blackcurrant jam.

It was time for the secret weapon… DNA.

One of DNA's pioneers, Professor Sir Alec Jeffreys at Leicester University, agreed to test the sample to find out from which animal it had emanated. After spending a couple more hours in a fridge at the Zoo, while onward transfer arrangements were made, it was on its way to Leicester, which, coincidently, was where it had come from in the first place.

It was an expensive, well-travelled round trip for a Thermos flask of what we hoped would be Big Cat Shit (from now on referred to as BCS). It would be a month before we obtained the results of the DNA from the BCS.

Pathetic though it might be to some, waiting for news was as exciting as waiting for my exam results when I was at school. I was standing on the precipice of discovery even greater than investigations into the existence of the Loch Ness Monster. No one had ever found a sample of LNMS and had it DNA'd, had they?

Sheepdog

It was little wonder that when the news was made public, television cameras, press photographers, journalists and radio stations were all waiting to receive it.

Robin Oakley from BBC television was first to arrive, closely followed by ITV, Discovery Channel and Sky News, which were ready to beam the news to the world. I intended to make the official announcement outside the puma enclosure, where our pumas made a dramatic backdrop for the momentous occasion.

Expectations were running high that the sample belonged to a big cat from the wilds of Leicester. My stage props were at the ready. I had some fresh puma faeces in a jar that Cheski had collected from the pumas' enclosure, and a plaster cast of a paw print that had been taken some time ago. It was a big one.

Paw print cast and puma droppings.

I was asked to hold the jar of BCS near to my face, and hold the plaster cast in the other hand, so that everyone would know what we had been examining to prove the existence of big cats in the wild in Britain.

The world was watching me.

Then I told the world that the BCS was not from a big cat. At that moment I wished I was anywhere but where I was. A colleague of Professor Sir Alec Jeffreys, Dr Esther Signer, who carried out the DNA analysis on the sample, informed me that the analysis proved that the faeces came from a sheep. Its texture and appearance had been moulded by a passing dog relieving itself on it. It appears that my man from The Midlands had seen a big dog peeing on SS, which accounted for the fact that it had still been warm when he touched it.

Disappointing it definitely was, but it made a good story and good viewing. Despite the setback, investigations would continue. People were afraid of the possibility of being attacked by a big cat, and farmers, quite rightly, were worried about attacks on their animals.

It was reaching the stage where most animals' deaths, caused through injuries, were blamed on big cats, and some of the attacks to which I was called were pretty horrific. But few were typical cat kills.

I was once called to look at a horse that had deep cuts on its hind quarters. The farmer thought the cuts looked like claw marks, and he was right, but they were not caused by a big cat. The horse had been attacked in a field where the boundary was a stone hedge. The night of the attack had been wet and windy, so it was likely that the horse, in order to find shelter, had been standing next to the hedge. Close investigation revealed that the top of the hedge had been flattened in one place, and either side of it was a narrow, well-worn path. The trampled grass beneath this flattened area indicated that it was where the horse had been standing.

The well-worn path was a typical badger 'run'. Badgers don't enjoy brilliant sight, and tend to stick to a particular familiar route on their nightly hunting expeditions. It was likely that a badger had followed the path and climbed the hedge, but instead of clambering down to the ground as was usual, it had landed on the back of the horse which was sheltering from the bad weather. The frightened horse bolted, and the equally frightened badger dug in its claws to hold on before it slid unceremoniously to the ground and lumbered off into the night. The cuts were more typical of badger claw marks than a big cat, and further evidence – tracks and hair – substantiated this.

Then there was another call, which was much more serious. A horse and its foal had been badly cut, and the cuts were evident mostly on shoulders and rumps. At first glance they looked like they had been caused by claws or barbed wire, but they were not claw marks, nor were they caused by barbed wire.

I contacted the police, because they had been caused by knives. They were not jagged tears of uneven force; they were straight slices that had been done with even force and had all the hallmarks of sharp knife slashes. It was a sad reflection of the mindless and cruel behaviour of some people.

*

If, as sometimes happened, I got a call saying that a whole flock of sheep had been attacked, I immediately dismissed the possibility of a big cat being responsible. A cat hunts for food, and hunts alone. While it would have killed one sheep after singling it out, the others, aware of the intruder, would have fled in terror.

I encountered this problem when three sheep had had their wool pulled away and their skins had been severely clawed and bitten. 'I'm sure it was a big cat,' the farmer told me. Two of three had their stomachs torn out, and were lying dead in the field, while one had made it to the safety of the farmyard in a badly traumatized state.

It was the work of dogs. Dogs are pack animals; the scent of blood and panicking sheep work them into an excited frenzy of destruction, which would cause the damage I witnessed on that farm. The myriad different size paw prints I found bore claw marks, indicating that there were probably at least four dogs. It was not simply food they were after; it was the thrill of the kill. Dogs among a flock of sheep can do a lot of harm.

A sheep attacked by dogs.

But not all sheep kills I was called to were caused by dogs. One in particular convinced me it was the work of a big cat. Jack Tarr, a police wildlife liaison officer, and I had been called to a farm near Falmouth, where we were shown a dead lamb in a corner of a field next to a hedge. It hadn't been killed there; the scene of the kill was in the middle of the field, evidenced by the blood and strands of wool we found there. The lamb's body had been dragged to the corner, which provided relative cover for the cat while it ate. We also found pointed claw marks where it had been digging. Since the carcass was too heavy to drag far, it would have been buried and dug up later.

The Rising Phoenix

Nice to See You

Cinnamon with Jenny.

Holidays are most welcome, but I missed the excitement of the Zoo. It wasn't just a job, it was a way of life; one that was forever changing. There were births, deaths, arrivals and departures, and my staff regularly said hello and waved goodbye. I wanted to be there when they did.

Before going on holiday, I said hello to two baby otters. The parent otters, Mike and Jenny, already had a youngster, Cinnamon, so-named because of her blonde colour, which was caused by a deficient gene. She was an attractive otter, but her colour was not the most desirable for survival in the wild, where she would have stood out in a crowd and been easy prey to hungry otter-lovers. She was destined eventually to go to another zoo, so two new babies were welcome additions to the family.

For the first month at least, baby otters' skins are not waterproof. They need mother's milk and the warmth of the nest. Cinnamon had other ideas, being of the opinion that otters, regardless of age, needed to swim.

Holding each of them in her teeth by the scruff of their necks, she carried them and lowered them into the water, which was where two little otters drowned. There was probably a period of mourning for the parents, but they were likely to recover before the keeper who looked after them. For him, the births were a triumph that had been turned into a disaster.

Animals are more resilient than humans, and there will probably be more baby otters in time. But no one liked saying goodbye in this way.

*

Two of our strangest and most welcome guests were fossas – cat-like animals found only in Madagascar. Due to deforestation, these creatures, together with lemurs, birds, insects and reptiles which shared the Madagascan forests with them, are on the endangered list. Breeding in zoos was desirable to ensure the continuation and safety of the species.

They are partial to guinea fowl, and it had not gone unnoticed that our free-ranging guinea fowl no longer passed by their enclosure on their daily travels. Fossas are predominantly solitary and nocturnal, but ours were happy to be seen together at any time. They were a couple of diurnal fossas.

Fo

But while Jenny and I had been in Africa, there had been births of cotton-top tamarin twins, which were being well looked after by Dad, three raccoons and a Sulawesi crested macaque monkey. One raccoon had died of old age, and a macaque, anxious to assert his dominance within the group, suffered an injury at the hands of Hemlock, the alpha male.

The staff had also waved goodbye to a young male Diana monkey, whose bloodline had been acceptable to a young female in France, while a white peacock, hell-bent on suicide, flew into the lion enclosure and provided Ronnie and Lizzie with an unexpected enrichment opportunity. The next day, all that was left was a sack full of white feathers. It's a fragile world.

Where Have all the Cows Gone?

Just how fragile is our world we discovered when, early in 2001 an outbreak of foot and mouth disease, which affects cloven-hoofed animals, was discovered on a farm in the South West of England.

Soon, the whole country had become affected by this contagious disease, which had been spread by the movement of livestock from farms to markets and back to farms. The rapid spread of what had previously been an isolated case, resulted in a gentle breeze becoming a hurricane that devastated Britain.

To put it into perspective, the disease in itself was not fatal. It was curable, or at the very least containable by vaccination. However, the effect of vaccination could mean that meat and animal stocks would have a reduced value, which would be economically disastrous to farming and related industries.

The irresponsible way in which the matter was handled by the government had much the same effect, and many businesses suffered economic disaster and never recovered. Government departments, some of which had no experience of such a problem, seemed unable to cope. 'Chaos' and 'disorganization' were words used to describe some of the decisions made and actions taken and, as a result, panic and confusion spread almost as quickly as the disease itself.

Infected animals and those suspected but not infected, were slaughtered. Throughout Britain, burning bonfires of bodies sent blackened smoke skywards. Many fit and well animals died needlessly. We were told that such a precaution was necessary to eradicate the disease. Memories of the scenes of carnage will remain, not only as a reminder of foot and mouth, but as a reminder of bungling bureaucracy.

I would not deny the seriousness of the epidemic, nor the need for swift action to avoid it spreading. Some of the measures taken undoubtedly helped contain it, especially restricting farm-animal movements; isolation of areas known to be infected, and regular disinfection of traffic and people that came into contact with infected areas and animals.

Unfortunately, the whole of Britain became a 'no go' area at a time when the country was preparing for the tourist season. Britain was getting ready to go as people were about to take holidays. Apart from the economic disaster faced by farmers, many businesses relied on tourists for their survival. Many closed, never to reopen.

The media didn't help by putting fear of foot and mouth into people, and those who didn't understand the nature of the disease became frightened by what they'd seen and heard in the press and on television. A group of adults who had booked a visit to the Zoo cancelled in case they caught foot and mouth. Irrationality took over rational thought and behaviour.

Dogs were allowed out in public only on leads, but cats, foxes, hedgehogs, badgers, birds and every other wild animal wandered freely wherever they wished. Dogs on leads were banned from paths near the Zoo. I couldn't understand this logic.

The local council laid a large strip of carpet at the entrance to the Zoo car-park, which was then soaked with disinfectant. The idea, definitely a good one, meant vehicles would have their wheels disinfected to avoid transferring the disease. This procedure happened all over Britain. Disinfecting would help to contain the problem, and in time eradicate the disease.

A month later though, the carpet was still there. Hundreds of cars had passed over it; it had been rained upon many times; dogs had probably peed on it, but I never saw it disinfected again. I remember it well: it had a floral pattern, full of red and yellow swirls, the sort often found in hotels. One of my staff suggested we should hoover it.

Such road decoration was typical of the many futile gestures that were made at this crucial time, and eventually, despite its pretty appearance at the entrance to the Zoo car park, we removed the carpet and burned it to avoid the possibility of spreading any number of diseases.

Tourists who were about 'to go' stopped going. Hotels, holiday parks and restaurants closed; public transport became a rarity, and private transport was discouraged unless essential.

Someone of great importance in government declared it was a war against a disease. It was a war alright, but the battle was not going to plan. Foot and mouth still spread, and bonfires still burned.

At the Zoo there were deer, sheep, zebu, capybara, llama, goats and pigs, all of which had cloven hooves, and all were suspects. Most zoos had some cloven-hoofed animals and, as a result, most zoos, including Newquay, closed to the public.

For us, the time we remained closed was a drain on our limited financial resources. Animals had to be cared for; food had to be bought; wages had to be paid, as did rates and utilities. These commitments now had to be met without income. Without the comfort of cash generation, it became difficult to face the future with confidence, and any development plans had to be put on hold.

All but one of my staff agreed to work for half pay, because they weren't prepared to walk away from the animals to which they had made personal commitments. Some, who were not directly involved with animals, also chose to work for half pay, since the Zoo operation relied on them too. The one who decided to leave did so, because, having a large family, his whole wage was 'budgeted for'. His bottom line was the breadline, and without his wage he would be on it. I wondered if anyone in government understood such desperation.

Foot and mouth disease was a problem that was with us, but organized thought, competent leadership and action was sadly lacking, and this situation did little to lessen the force of its impact.

People and businesses suffered; prize herds of cattle were slaughtered; milk yields were affected, and important bloodlines disappeared in smoke, never to be replaced. While the bovine population was being depleted, deer roamed the forests, and other animals and birds wandered through the countryside, even through infected areas. There were no means of preventing them from doing so.

Keeping dogs on leads, and leaving pretty carpets without disinfectant on roads, were merely ways of paying lip service to satisfy those in authority who continued to panic. Vaccination was still high on my list of priorities. We were told that supplies of the vaccine were available, should a decision in favour of it be made.

In some countries, foot and mouth disease is endemic, and vaccination is used to control it, so why were we being so hesitant, especially since we still purchased meat from these countries?

I didn't want to enter into an argument which would be counterproductive to the future of farming, but, given the chaos that was happening throughout the country, there didn't seem to be much future anyway. Furthermore, if the sole argument was about contaminated meat having less value as a marketable product, why were zoo animals not vaccinated? Zoos' cloven-hoofed animals did not enter the food chain; were not sold on the open market, and did not travel anywhere without a full 'MOT'.

To travel even short distances, they would have to be free of disease. There would have been no possibility of it being transmitted, especially if no direct contact with infected animals had ever occurred. But no one was exempt, everyone was suspected.

During our closure, Jenny and I went to Devon for a few days to a country hotel. When the owner of the hotel saw 'Newquay Zoo' written on our vehicle, it soon became apparent we were not welcome. We were pariahs in their midst. 'Why not come another time?' we were asked.

'We want to come now,' we said. Footbaths were hurriedly placed at the doorway, and we got the impression that we were being avoided. We were pleased that the waiter refrained from wearing a face-mask when serving us at dinner. It was a very disinfecting few days.

Walking over the moors and visiting villages, antique shops and tea rooms was our way of recharging our batteries in readiness for the decisions of the day-job. Luckily, a couple of weeks later, we found the Lord

Haldon Hotel. It was on the edge of Dartmoor, near several small villages, a short distance from the city of Exeter, and we were not avoided or inspected for foot and mouth disease.

Indeed, we were made very welcome by the owners, Michael and Laurie Preece, experienced hoteliers who ran their hotel with elegance and style. They created a sort of Fawlty Towers atmosphere of informality and friendliness, which immediately put their guests at ease. However, the organization was anything but Fawlty Towers-ish, and oozed professionalism. Good customer care, sadly lacking in some hotels, was a priority at the Lord Haldon. It became our battery-charger, and Michael and Laurie became close friends.

*

This was a time when people needed friends, and not feel unwanted, so when I received a phone call from a head teacher wanting to bring his school to the Zoo, even though it was closed, I was pleased to welcome him. Our country needed cheering up, so we cheered up a school.

We took all precautions: shoes were disinfected in the many disinfection baths located around the Zoo, and we laid a new strip of carpet along the road for the coach to pass over. It was light green, looked like grass, and was soaked in disinfectant. We kept it in position for some time after the visit, and disinfected it daily to help the war effort.

The children had a wonderful day, and so did the animals. Animals like people. Best of all, no one caught foot and mouth disease.

But the war continued; so did our closure, and my concern at the damage being done to local businesses was raised by our MP, Matthew Taylor, in the House of Commons. I and other business people wrote letters to newspapers, to MAFF, and to any organization fighting the battle, but all protestations and concerns fell on deaf ears. There was no noticeable reaction.

However, my concern did come to the attention of some people. I was in my office when Dave Alexander, entertainments manager at a local hotel, came in carrying a large bag. 'We've had a raffle, a quiz night, a karaoke evening and a tombola game at the hotel to help the Zoo during the foot and mouth crisis.' With that, he emptied a large bag of money on to the desk.

Dave's was the first of many donations we received. There were collection boxes in petrol stations, supermarkets, shops, offices and hotels… all destined for the Zoo. Celia Springett, a close neighbour, who is disabled, did a sponsored walk; Sir Ray Tindle, owner of a newspaper group, made a substantial donation, and many people arrived with food for the animals. Newquay was the people's zoo, foot and mouth disease wasn't going to close it.

*

Ronnie and Connie.

One day, he came into the office and handed me a cheque, looked me in the eye, and said, 'Connie would want me to give this to you. She said, when I go, Freddy, I want to leave something for our lions.'

Fred thought this was the time to do it, since Ronnie needed a friend, just like he did. It was a generous donation from them both and would pay for the vet's fees, Comet's transportation from Longleat, a new platform in the enclosure, and enough food for some time to come.

The new platform was completed in time for Comet's arrival in a trailer pulled by a Land Rover driven by Bob Trollope. He called Newquay Zoo 'The Lions of Longleat Annex'. Unfortunately, he and Keith had to get back to Longleat, so were unable to stay to see father and daughter meet a few days later.

A television crew from BBC Spotlight; Radio Cornwall; a press photographer; our vet; Fred; Roger Martin and his new wife and I were at the reunion. So were two off-duty firemen who had 'come to watch and have a cup of coffee'.

We didn't have a rehearsal, and when the automatic door opened, Ronnie bounded out, roaring. Comet came over to him, and after some sniffing, they nuzzled each other. The day before they met, we had changed Comet's name, and her new name was displayed on a mounted brass plaque outside the enclosure.

That's how Ronnie met Connie, and from their behaviour I was certain that they recognized each other. She would be good company for her dad, and Fred could come and chat to Connie whenever he wanted.

After the family reunion, we all went to the café where I was introduced to Joanne. Roger and she had had a quiet wedding, with just family. It was the only one of Roger's weddings that I hadn't been invited to.

While he'd been getting married, going on honeymoon and moving house, so much had happened that I needed to share the exciting news with him. Newquay Junior School's football field backed on to the Zoo. It was so wet from springs that it was mostly under water, and would have made a better swimming pool than a football pitch. It would be perfect as a wetland centre about British wildlife, to add to the Zoo's

Open day at the college, with Mike Kent.

attractions, so I negotiated the lease and planned for its future. However, not all plans come to fruition.

We had had our application for extension of the main zoo lease to ninety-nine years approved by Restormel Borough Council, so future investment could be safely made without risk. The council was pleased that under our ownership Newquay Zoo had prospered and was a credit to the county. We could 'stay as long as we wanted'.

Things were falling into place at last, and when the seed that Mike Kent and I had planted many years ago became a flower, our dream became a reality. Newquay Zoo's college, now completed, had become an important Environmental Study Centre for the new Combined Universities of Cornwall. Those first students, who had studied for much of their course in temporary rented accommodation that I had secured, now worked in a state-of-the-art college. The first graduation ceremony took place in Truro Cathedral.

Jenny and I, guests of honour, walked to our seats in the Cathedral in procession with the Chancellor, other VIPs and university staff. It was a proud, emotional time being present at a prestigious educational ceremony which I had been instrumental in creating.

Visitors from the Sky

Since we had removed cotton-top tamarins from the freedom of the 'forest', the tree house had been unoccupied. Wishing to capitalize on what had been a successful experiment, we repeated 'wild living' with black lemurs.

Lemurs look like monkeys, but are in fact a species of their own, and there are many subspecies of these interesting mammals, of different sizes and colours. They are found only in the forests of Madagascar.

At Newquay Zoo, there were red-ruffed lemurs; gentle lemurs; rin tailed lemurs, and black lemurs. The latter were moved to the tree hc

Lemur feeding time.

in the wood. While some of the lemur species are now extinct in Madagascar, we had successfully bred black lemurs, and intended to continue to do so in line with the Zoo Federation's policy.

When we took the group off their island home, where they had lived very contentedly ever since Exotic Clive made them a forest, they were locked in the house for a week's familiarization period. Being creatures of habit, and needing security, when let out they readily returned at feeding times. We and they were happy that all was going to plan.

On cold days in winter, they wouldn't want to venture far, preferring the warmth of the tree house. But now, although early autumn, it was still warm in the daytime, and the area of woodland was an exciting place to find fruit which we had hidden in nooks and crannies in the trees.

Our lemurs had not heard of the Red Arrows aerobatic flying team, who gave displays world-wide and often practised from nearby RAF St Mawgan. Planes at the base didn't fly over the Zoo, in order not to frighten the animals; their flight paths followed the coastline before heading out to sea.

The Red Arrows, however, were not aware of this. While they flew north out over the sea, the lemurs were enjoying the freedom of the 'forest'. When the Red Arrows turned, in their well-recognized formation, they flew over the Zoo.

To our visitors it was a wonderful sight, but the lemurs thought they were being attacked. Frightened, they fled in every direction, which for was beyond the Zoo perimeter. Keepers armed with bowls of fruit managed to persuade them to return. Peace was restored, until... 'The Return of the Red Arrows': this time, in the same recognized formation, but leaving trails of coloured smoke behind.

The lemurs had had enough. First the noise, and now the noise and coloured smoke. Off they went. It took staff an hour to locate them, and much longer to pacify five nervously wrecked lemurs. To ease

Red Arrows fly in signing up Red Lemur Eleven.

their troubled minds, they were not put back in the tree house, but taken to the island home where they had previously lived happily in a really nasty-tasting rainforest. There were to be no more shocks.

I notified Squadron Leader Dave Webster at St Mawgan about the incident. He, in turn, spoke to the Red Arrows, who were mortified to hear they had frightened our lemurs. The Zoo was not indicated on their map, so they'd had no idea of the problem that had been caused.

Just before afternoon feeding time, Red One, Squadron Leader 'Spike' Jepson and some of his team arrived bearing gifts and, by way of an apology, helped feed the lemurs, which were now in the safety of their island home. The way to a lemur's heart is via its stomach. Food means sorry.

Although they are called black lemurs, only the males are black; the females are rusty red. The Red Arrows made lemur friends that day, and decided to adopt one of them. Red Lemur Eleven became a Red Arrow, the first female to join the flying squadron. Afterwards, Spike and his colleagues joined our visitors for tea on the patio; signed autographs; gave out copies of the Red Arrows brochure, and informally chatted about their work.

The report of their visit and the latest recruit to the Squadron was shown on television that evening, and featured in newspapers the following day. All was forgiven.

*

'You'll be surprised,' Geoff said.

I was. Having reached a mature age, he had decided to embrace senior citizenship by retiring. I had first met one of my most trusted managers and good friend more than nine years ago when he was on sentry duty at the Zoo. Newquay's 'jewel in the crown' owed much to him.

He didn't leave until after our ninth Animals Carol Service, where visitors, and animals in stalls made of hay, gathered under heaters on the patio to celebrate the occasion. The Revd Peter Long was thrilled to have such a large congregation, and especially delighted to see that some of them had horns and tails.

The Zoo had become profitable, and we were free of any financial constraints, so when the New Year dawned, our tenth, we were able to plan for the future with confidence.

Bangers and Mash

For three days in May 2003, we became the focus of attention of zoo directors, curators and environmentalists throughout Britain and Ireland. We hosted the Annual Conference of The National Federation of Zoos (now BIAZA – British and Irish Association of Zoos and Aquaria), an accolade normally reserved for larger and longer-established zoos. We had achieved recognition. Newquay Zoo had come of age.

Hotel accommodation for eighty delegates from sixty-seven zoos; places of interest to visit; workshops; guest speakers, and a farewell dinner on the final night had been organized… and rehearsed many times. I was an obsessive rehearser.

The three-day event was marred only by the weather. Rain and thick sea mist descended the moment the reception party began on the open-air patio overlooking the lake. In good weather, it would have provided an exciting venue and a wonderful welcome to the Zoo. However, raincoats, umbrellas and the café awning prevented the dampening of spirits, and it didn't take long for good conversation and laughter to prevail in the warmth of good company.

The customary sausages and cheese cubes on sticks, sandwiches, pasties and rain-diluted glasses of wine heralded a happy introduction to the conference. Many of the delegates had asked for and been given sea views from their rooms. Unfortunately, Cornish mist is no respecter of sea views. Very few saw the sea that weekend.

The next two days were packed with fascinating lectures, workshops, forums and sightseeing trips. The final night dinner was held at The Eden Project, where our selected menu was a trio of sausages and creamed potatoes. The dinner ended with me thanking the delegates for their presence, and their toleration of the Cornish Riviera weather in May. The British weather is always a good talking point.

The conference ended the following morning with a guided tour of the Zoo, before the AGM took place in our new college lecture room. It was a wonderful opportunity to show off our state-of-the-art college.

After an early lunch, the delegates made their way home to their respective zoos throughout the country; but not before they looked seawards, with one desperate hope. There were ships out there; we could hear the foghorns. In spite of the weather, the press got some good photographs, and the next day in our local paper there were eighty smiling faces.

ever seen – collected him. It was the start of a new adventure, with new friends. Although we intended to visit him often, the day of his departure was not a happy one.

There were others who noticed his absence. My grandchildren, Toby, Archie, Barney and Kitt, all asked the same question when they visited us. 'Where's Cyril, Grandpa?' I showed them a photograph of his first Christmas at The Donkey Sanctuary.

So much of my life had been spent in the company of animals. Holly told Jen about the time I kept pigs when we lived on a farm. 'I'll never forget watching Dad castrate the piglets.' Nor would I. It was the most painful process I'd ever been through, and not only for the pigs.

All our family, except me, had stuck to two professions… education and design. Jenny, her daughter Jo, Holly and I, were, or had been, teachers. Ben is an architect, Holly's husband, Dave, and Ben's wife, Francesca, are both teachers. Jo's future husband, Jamie, is a designer.

I took a few diversions along the way. I had been: a teacher; a manufacturer of spiral stairways; a designer; a managing director of a seal sanctuary; and the owner of a zoo.

Not many can say that.

It has been an interesting life, so far. Jenny said I ought to write a book about it. I was going to be an author.

 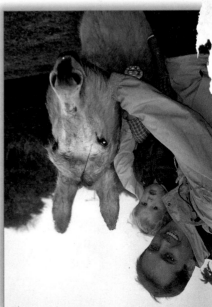

…en and his son, Archie, with Cyril at Cott Farm (left). Cyril in festive mood at The Donkey Sanctuary in Sidmouth (right).

Back to the Future

Beginning at the End

When the time came to make another major decision, it was not easy. The brown, pebbledash cottage with blue window frames that I first saw as I drove along the road to Gweek twenty-two years ago, was a short distance from where I now sat at the bottom of the garden.

The sounds of the stream and evening owls kept me company. The resident pair of buzzards, which nested in a beech tree in the orchard, circled overhead, and pipistrelle bats, which lived in the attic, whirled around and swooped inches from my face. They are the Red Arrows of the night.

It was fascinating to watch them in flight, looking for their insect dinner. Although their sight is almost as good as humans', at night they rely on a special sonar system of echoes caused by their shouts, which are generally too high-pitched for humans to hear. I listened, but heard nothing.

The pheasants, which we fed daily, had taken cover for the night, but woodpeckers seeking their evening meal drilled into the nearby oak trees to flush out insects as the sinking sun quenched its rays and darkness welcomed the foragers of the night... badgers and foxes. Animals, birds and insects were our neighbours.

Cott Farm is no longer pebbledash with blue window frames. It seemed to smile as the evening shadows moved slowly over the white-painted walls, stretching its image across the lawn towards me.

Nick and Gingerman had lived most of their lives at Cott, and they always will. They are buried in the orchard. It had been a kind home, a comfortable, good friend. I would miss this world.

But another world was about to open its doors to Jenny and me. It had sea views, and was in Falmouth, a hundred yards from the beach and a short walk from Wellington Terrace, the school where I last taught. It's true that teachers retire to a cottage by the sea.

It's a small house with a very small garden, and humans are our neighbours, but there is no field. Donkeys need a field. Some months earlier, in preparation for our move, Cyril went to The Donkey Sanctuary in Sidmouth. His taxi – the most luxurious animal transporter I have

Zoo One off radio.

With Jenny (left), and Roger (right) at the leaving party.

What I hadn't told anyone at the conference was that we were in negotia-
tions to sell the Zoo. Selling had not been an easy decision to make, since,
despite the many difficulties, it had been the happiest decade of my life.
I was happily married; made many good friends, and had a successful
business working with children and animals. So far, my ambition had
been fulfilled.

Operating a zoo was running a business unlike any other. It was not
possible to turn off the lights, lock the gates and go home. It needed
twenty-four hours a day, three hundred and sixty-five days a year of care
and supervision. For ten years, we had cared for animals; educated children; entertained visitors, and looked after our community and our staff.
We were also shopkeepers and café proprietors.

I remember the early days, when we only had six staff, thirty-six thousand visitors a year, and a bank balance that didn't. In fact, it tilted so
dramatically the wrong way that personal disaster had loomed around
every corner. Those were the days when Jenny and I ran the shop; helped
Geoff in reception; assisted in the café; ran the office; helped with the site
cleaning, and did the café laundry at home in the evenings. Jenny, as well
as being the shop manager, with the help of her mother made cakes for
the café. I did all the public talks at feeding times.

There were times when there were few people to talk to, but one person was as important as five hundred, so I never refrained from doing it.
We recalled those days with fondness. We had faced the challenge and
enjoyed it. We believed in what we were doing; we overcame the difficulties, and succeeded. In many ways, those days were as enjoyable and
just as happy as those ten years later when we had forty-five staff; two
hundred and fifty thousand visitors a year, and money in the bank. We
inherited a puddle, and created a lake.

Geoff had retired. Mike Pulley, our long-suffering bank manager,
was about to, and I was getting older while the Zoo was getting busier – a
recipe for incompatibility. As custodians we had enjoyed a good relationship with our landlord, Restormel Council, and special help and friendship
from councillors John Weller, Joan Vincent and Norman Thompson. The
support and friendship of so many people in Newquay saw us through
the days of difficulty, and will always have a place in our hearts. When the
time came to go, Jenny, Roger and I had been on a great adventure.
The Whitley Wildlife Trust, owners of Paignton Zoo, would hopefully
be worthy successors, which was why I was in Paignton to sign the com-
pletion of sale document on behalf of me and Roger. He was at home,
nursing a broken ankle.

The elation of selling a successful business that, almost ten years ago,
was in danger of closing due to lack of visitors and finance, was, in part,
tempered by leaving it. We were leaving a good friend.
There was one regret. I never did create the Wetland Centre for British
Wildlife. But we had owned a zoo. Not many can say that.

*